Pewter Craft

Sandy Griffiths

Pewter Craft

FIREFLY BOOKS

A FIREFLY BOOK

Published by Firefly Books Ltd. 2010
Copyright © 2010 Metz Press

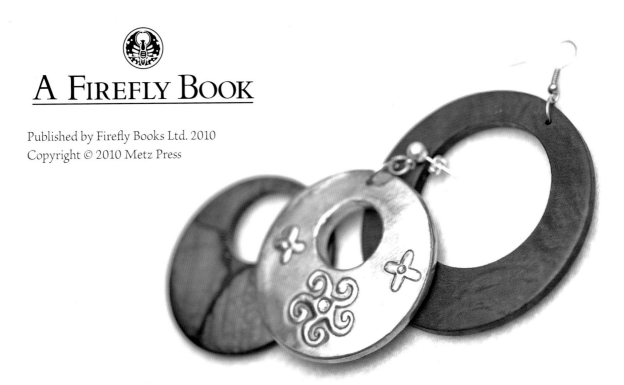

First printing

Publisher Cataloging-in-Publication Data (U.S.)
Griffiths, Sandy.
    Pewter craft / Sandy Griffiths.
[144] p. : col. photos. ; cm.
Summary: Numerous projects with instructions, templates, and photographs,
range from jewelry to décor items.
ISBN-13: 978-1-55407-603-1 (pbk.)
ISBN-10: 1-55407-603-X (pbk.)
1. Pewtercraft. I. Title.
739.533 dc22   TT266.3.G754   2010

Library and Archives Canada Cataloguing in Publication
A CIP record of this book is available from Library and Archives Canada

Published in the United States by
Firefly Books (U.S.) Inc.
P.O. Box 1338, Ellicott Station
Buffalo, New York 14205

Published in Canada by
Firefly Books Ltd.
66 Leek Crescent
Richmond Hill, Ontario L4B 1H1

Printed in China

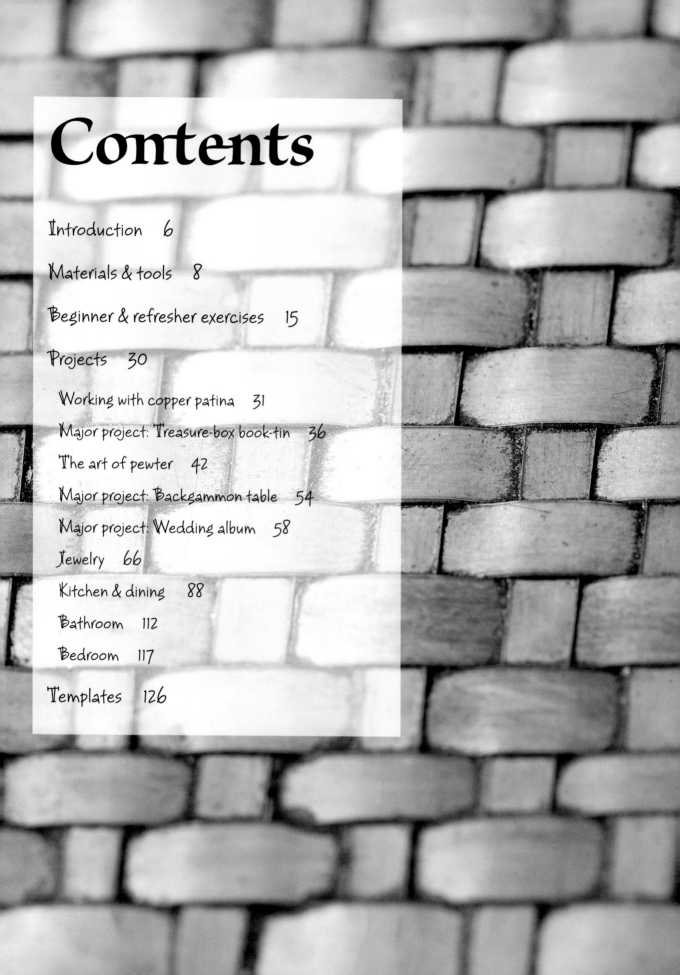

Contents

Introduction

When explaining to people that I work with pewter, one of the most frequently asked questions is, "What do you put pewter on?" However, before I can start rambling on, describing every item and article that I have ever covered with pewter, my husband usually pipes up and answers, "If it stands still long enough, you can pewter it."

If you are reading this, my guess is you have already decided to have fun, so relax and enjoy the book. I have written it in the form of a workshop and it is scattered with crafter's notes, which I hope will answer all your questions and give you some alternative methods that might work better for you. Mistakes will be made along the way but this is good — your mistakes are your best teachers. One of the reasons I am qualified to write this book is that I have probably made more mistakes than most. I like to call this experience.

Pewter is a series of techniques, so you don't have to be artistic or have any experience with other crafts — once you have learned the techniques you can apply them to various designs.

You do not have to be able to draw your own designs but it's an added bonus if you can. Having said that, it's very easy to trace designs from pictures in magazines, on greeting cards, in design books and so on. These designs can then be resized on a photocopier to fit the item you are wanting to pewter, but please bear in mind the copyright laws if you are working for commercial gain.

THE DIFFERENCES

There is a difference between pewter relief modeling, which is explained in this book, and cast pewter. Pewter relief modeling is used for decorative purposes and is done on thin sheets of pewter. The design is modeled from the back, using special tools, to create a raised or relief design on the front. The back is then filled with beeswax to prevent the soft metal from being flattened and the front is treated with a chemical called patina to give the metal an aged effect. The completed design is secured to a firm surface, which supports the pewter.

Cast pewter is a completely different craft. It is very intensive and requires melting down the pewter and pouring it into moulds to make items such as wine goblets, bowls, serving spoons, etc. (you might be familiar with Carrol Boyes' cast pewter work).

The teaspoon caddy on page 104 is created by weaving strips of pewter. This is an exciting project, as the technique is not part of traditional pewter relief nor anything like cast pewter, which just goes to show that you need to keep your imagination wide open. If you have an idea, experiment, try it out and, who knows, it might just work.

The information in this book is everything I know about the craft of pewter. This is not to say that I know everything about the craft, but I have shared all my current knowledge and I know I will keep learning more.

The price of pewter may be quoted by the piece, by length or by weight, and may initially seem quite high. Consider the cost of a single project, however, and you will be pleasantly surprised to find that pewter craft is no more expensive than any other hobby, so don't be put off by the price. Go forth, have fun and create wonderful projects. Call in sick from work, hide from family and friends and just pewter, pewter, pewter. Remember — if it stands still, there really is a good chance you can pewter it.

HOW TO USE THIS BOOK

Read through the chapter on materials and tools. There is a lot of information about the various materials and tools you will use while pursuing the art of pewter. This information will help you to purchase the right ones, as well as understand how to use the items safely and correctly.

I strongly advise you to work through all four of the beginner's exercises as they are designed specifically to teach you the techniques. I have separated the beginner's low-relief projects and high-relief projects so you may concentrate on learning one technique at a time. These projects are also handy if you have not done pewter for a while and your techniques are a little rusty, as they act as great refresher courses. Don't be frustrated if some of the techniques take a while at the beginning. They require practice and patience, so relax and enjoy the process and after a few attempts you will get the hang of it.

Once you have worked through the beginner's exercises, you can move onto any of the designs you wish to complete. The African angel and Samson & Delilah projects, on page 43, are good places to put all the techniques together, as is the Treasure-box book-tin on page 36.

Feel free to improvise and adapt any of the projects to suit both your personal taste and the object you wish to adorn with pewter. You will find the templates of all the designs in the back of the book, and they can be resized on a photocopier to fit your specific project.

Materials & tools

Take heart, you do not need loads of tools for the craft of pewter, and most of the tools you *do* need will last you a lifetime — I have students who work with their grandparents' tools. Many of the materials used are common household products, readily available from your local supermarket. One of the advantages of this craft is that the tools and materials required fit comfortably into a medium-size box or a beautiful pewter-adorned tin.

PEWTER SHEETS

These are thin sheets made up of lead, tin and a little copper. The more tin in the makeup, the shinier the pewter. Most manufacturers place a thin layer of tin over the sheet to make it shiny, and if you polish the pewter extensively this layer of tin may be rubbed off, exposing the layer underneath.

Lead-free pewter is becoming more readily available. Interestingly, this is a contradiction in terms, as, technically speaking, if there is no lead in the mix it is not pewter, but this is not something we need to worry about.

Most of the pewter available has a right side and a wrong side, and the right side is not necessarily the shiny side. Compare the back with the front: the back has a bluish tint while the front is whiter. The "non-technical" way of telling the difference is simply by looking at the roll. All pewter comes in rolls: the inside of the roll is the wrong side while the outside of the roll is the right side. It's important to know the difference because the patinating and polishing process doesn't work well on the back, so if you're not sure, use a small piece of pewter as a tester.

Pewter is very soft and may easily be cut with a pair of scissors or a craft knife. Being a soft metal, it must always be mounted onto something hard to give it support: bottles, wooden boxes, beads, frames and tins are all suitable items. As mentioned in the Introduction, pewter is sold in a range of formats, and may be priced by size or by weight. The price of a large sheet of pewter may sound expensive, but most projects will only require a relatively small amount.

WORK SURFACE

You will need a smooth, non-textured, hard surface on which to work, such as a wooden board or piece of glass (I use the MDF — medium density fiberboard — place mats available from most decoupage supply stores). Ensure that you keep your work surface free from scratches and blobs of beeswax, as any texture on the board will be transferred to the pewter while working on it.

SOFT CLOTH

This is used when modeling the pewter. When you want the pewter to "push out," you work on the soft cloth. If you try to model the pewter on the hard surface it will remain flat, as it has nothing to mold into. Felt, yellow dust cloths and a chamois are good options, but, once again, avoid anything with texture. The depth of your

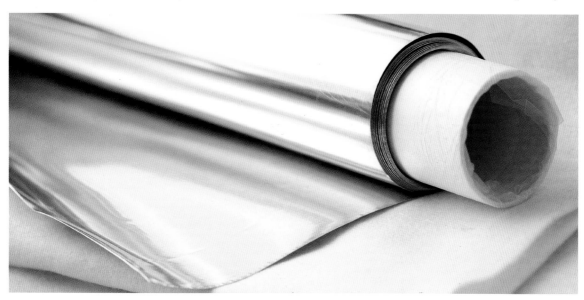

modeling will determine whether you need a single, double or triple layer of cloth. Always add one extra layer at a time (as needed) — if the layers of cloth are too thick, they won't provide enough support and the pewter will buckle.

LUBRICANT

When using tools on the pewter you will be working with metal on metal, and will therefore need a lubricant to help the tool move smoothly over the pewter. Without lubricant the tool will dig into the pewter, so use petroleum jelly, baby oil or cooking oil. The only time I don't use lubricant is when doing indented low-relief.

FILLER

This is used to fill in the back of a high-relief design to prevent the image from being pushed back or flattened. Beeswax works best, as it hardens quickly, does not contract when cold, and sticks to the pewter. Do not use candle wax as this contracts when cold and crumbles easily.

Heat the beeswax in an old jam jar until it is completely liquid. A glass dropper is then used to drop the beeswax into the back of the design. If the wax starts solidifying in the dropper while it is being sucked up it means it's not yet hot enough. Once you have filled the indentations, make sure that the wax is level with the flat, surrounding edges of the design. Any

wax outside the design must be cleaned off with turpentine on cotton wool. Do not be tempted to scratch it off with a tool or fingernail as you will scratch into the design. Never leave the wax unattended while heating as it is oil based and therefore flammable.

Be aware that hot wax attracts bees. Luckily, they have never stung me or my allergic students, but if you are afraid, take the tin of hot wax to an area away from where you are working and fill the design there, so that you don't have to spend too much time in their company (they will stay with the wax). If you're still a little

nervous, work when bees are unlikely to bother you — they are not active at night and seldom on cloudy, cold or rainy days.

Other materials that may be used to fill in the back of a high-relief design are modeling paste and premixed crack filler (add a water-based glue to the mixture). The premixed crack filler is a better option than the powdered variety that you mix yourself, as it does not contract as much. Fill the back of the design with the filler, ensuring that it is level with the pewter. Clean off any excess filler with a damp cloth. Allow 24 hours to dry.

GLASS DROPPERS

These are used to fill the back of the design with the beeswax. Glass droppers are inexpensive, and available at pharmacies. Work with at least two or three, as they will eventually clog up. When this happens, place the glass section into boiling water. Don't place the black rubber part into boiling water as it will perish; just pick out any cold wax with a tracer tool. Avoid turning the dropper upside down while it has hot wax inside it, as the wax will run back and clog your dropper.

PATINA

Patina is a liquid, chemical substance that has a corrosive effect on metal and is used on pewter to give it an antique, aged look. It also settles into the recesses of the design, which gives the design

depth. The longer the patina is left on, the more it darkens the pewter. If you find the patina is too strong and darkens the pewter too much, dilute the patina with water. To apply patina, absorb a little on a small piece of cotton wool and wipe evenly over the pewter.

When applying patina, wear protective gloves and be careful not to spill any onto your tools, as it will cause them to rust. If any spills occur, rinse off with clean water, as this neutralizes the effect of the patina.

Patina comes in two colors: black and copper. Black patina is normally used for the art of pewter. However, copper patina will also work, and results in a very interesting copper effect on the metal. The chemical reaction to the metal by the two

types of patina is very different (have a look at the spiral-bound book on page 31 for a project using both black and copper patina). If your local craft store doesn't stock patina, try a stained glass store or studio.

If you prefer a shinier, less aged look, leave out the patina, as it doesn't have to be used if you don't like the effect.

METAL POLISH

This is used to shine or buff the metal (whether you've used patina or not), which enhances the design. Any household metal polish will work. Apply with a piece of cotton wool, then buff using clean pieces of cotton wool.

Stove polish — available at supermarkets — is lovely to experiment with, as it also darkens the pewter and sits in the recesses

of the design. Use it instead of the patina or apply it afterward to enhance the effect.

MODELING TOOLS

Having the right tools makes it easier to achieve a professional finish. To work on pewter, you only need three specialized tools: a tracer, a paper pencil and a hockey-stick tool. Of course, having about three to four different size ball tools, and both large and small hockey sticks, is ideal, but you can quite comfortably do pewter work with only three tools.

Tracer This is used to trace the design onto the pewter for both high and low relief, and also to add very fine detail to your design. The tracer has a rounded tip similar to that of a knitting needle or a ballpoint pen. A tool with a

very small ball on the tip may also be used. Ensure that the tracer is not sharp, or it will cut through the pewter.

Paper pencil Also known as a torchon, this is used to flatten and neaten the areas around the modeled design. It is soft, so it will leave no scratches. It is also used as a modeling tool in areas of the design where the hockey stick is too large. The paper pencil is made of tightly rolled paper (similar to the paper stick on children's lollipops) with a sharpened point at each end. To clean or sharpen the paper pencil, rub the sides of the point on a piece of very fine sandpaper. After much use, the paper pencil will need to be replaced, but the old, flattened one makes a good modeling tool. I often use my old, very flat-topped paper pencil as

my hockey stick. It is a good idea to buy two paper pencils because then you can turn one of them into an "old, blunt" pencil by rubbing the pointy top on a piece of fine sandpaper to flatten it. Paper pencils are available at art stores as they're also used for blending chalk and oil pastels.

Hockey stick This is used to model the pewter when doing high relief. If you are doing a very large design, a teaspoon is perfect for the job. Always keep the tool at a low angle when modeling — only the rounded, middle part of the tool should touch the pewter. Don't let the front point or sides touch, as this creates grooves in your design. A small hockey stick is useful for modeling little areas of the design. If you don't have one, a paper pencil will work perfectly.

Ball tool This tool has a ball at the tip and is available in various sizes. It is used when doing low relief to make a broader design line than the tracer will produce. When you want to broaden a design line, always start with the tracer and then use a larger ball tool. Never start with the larger ball tool, as pewter should be stretched out slowly to prevent buckling. The ball tool is also used to create raised dots or small rounded areas on the pewter. However, be very careful not to push through the pewter when pushing out dots.

Sharp stylus The thin, pointed shape of this tool makes the cutting out of small, intricate areas a lot easier. However, a small pair of scissors or a craft knife and cutting mat will do the job most of the time.

GLUE

Any glue that is compatible with metal and the surface to which you are adhering the pewter will work, so inquire at your local hardware store. My glues of preference are the contact ones — the spray contact adhesive being my extravagant favorite. The choice depends on the project though. Most contact adhesives are quick drying, but need at least 24 hours to set properly. Do not use water-based glue on any item that will come into contact with water, as this dissolves the glue. You need to consider if the item will ever be washed or have condensation form on it. Clear epoxy glue is great for sticking beads and stones to the pewter.

Clean off excess water-based glue with a damp cloth. Most other glues can be cleaned off with turpentine or vinegar, but read the instructions on the glue.

COLORING AGENTS

Glass paints or stains These are normally used to create a stained-glass effect. I prefer working with brands that use acetone as a solvent rather than the water-based brands, as they are hardier and the colors richer. These paints are a good partner to pewter because they are made to adhere to nonabsorbent surfaces.

Metal-leaf papers These are available in gold, copper and silver. The metallic colors complement the pewter.

Gold and copper paint pens These are easy to work with and give similar results to metal leaf.

TRACING PAPER

Use good-quality tracing paper to transfer your designs — the thicker, 90 gsm tracing paper is best. If you try working with thin tracing paper, the tracing tool will probably cut through it when you trace the design onto the pewter. This is very distracting and normally results in the design being traced unevenly. When purchasing tracing paper, it is more economical to buy a 12" x 18" (or A3 size) pad, because this will also accommodate designs for larger projects.

RUBBER ROLLER

This is used to flatten out the pewter sheet when necessary.

BLANKS

Undecorated boxes, clocks, bottles, frames, tins and dishes are just some examples of items that can be used. Decoupage blanks are particularly suitable. Always ensure that your base is fully prepared before attaching the pewter — all painting, sanding and varnishing must be done beforehand.

SHAPE TEMPLATES

These are stencils of various mathematical shapes and come in ascending sizes. For example: circles, ovals, squares, hexagons, etc. Although not a must-have, they will prove to be invaluable, especially when doing circles and ovals, as these two shapes are particularly difficult to draw or trace perfectly. I place the templates directly onto the pewter and trace from them when using any of these shapes on my pewter designs. Just be aware that most of these templates have little raised bumps underneath, so when using them, turn them upside down to avoid the bumps pressing into the pewter. They are available at stationery, art and craft stores.

MISCELLANEOUS

You will need these for most of the projects:

Cotton wool to apply patina, for polishing and for cleaning — this will be used in large quantities.

Masking tape to secure designs to pewter while tracing.

Rubber or latex gloves to protect your hands when using patina.

Turpentine for cleaning off excess beeswax and glue.

Pencil and ruler.

Scissors — small, curved nail scissors are best for cutting out designs.

Craft knife and cutting mat or glass surface.

Beginner & refresher exercises

These designs have been created to take you through both high and low relief, the only two techniques required for the art of pewter. I suggest that you work through the four beginner's exercises before trying any of the designs further on in the book. They are uncomplicated, and this enables you to concentrate on the techniques rather than the designs themselves.

Practice them, master them and understand them. It will make your journey through the book far easier and a lot more fun. By understanding the different results of the techniques, you will gain the experience to decide how to tackle your own designs. You will also discover that it is the contrast of the techniques that adds interest to the pewter designs.

Low relief

Low relief may be done from the front or from the back of the pewter. If done from the front, the design will be indented and therefore hold more patina and polish, so the design lines will become black. If done from the back of the pewter, the design lines will be slightly raised (not high relief); they will not hold the patina and polish, and so will be shiny. I will take you through both indented and raised low-relief so you can master both techniques.

Heart 1 (indented low-relief)

Indented low-relief is a simple technique; it is almost like drawing on the front of the pewter to indent it slightly. Although the technique is fairly basic, the results are very effective because the polish sits dark in the indentations, creating an interesting contrast between the silver of the polished pewter and the black of the indentations. This is the technique used to create the Naked chefs salt and pepper grinders on page 108.

You will need

soft pencil (6B)
tracing paper
piece of pewter 2$\frac{3}{4}$" x 2$\frac{3}{4}$" (7 cm x 7 cm)
1 piece of felt
hard board
masking tape
tracer tool or small ball tool
materials for polishing (see page 24)

1. Trace the heart design from page 127. Place a single piece of felt onto the hard board and then put the pewter, right-side up, on top of the felt. Secure well with masking tape.

2. Place tracing-paper design onto the pewter. Center it and secure on all four sides with masking tape. This stops the design moving while you are tracing, preventing broken or double design lines.

3. Using the tracer tool or small ball tool, trace the entire design onto the pewter. Press harder than you would if writing.

4. Remove the tracing paper and masking tape. Rub over the pewter with your finger to flatten it.

5. The design is now indented into the pewter. If you are light handed, you may need to retrace the design, pressing harder this time — do this without the tracing paper. If you are happy with the depth of the design, do not retrace.

6. Polish the pewter. I will take you through the polishing process at the end of the beginner's exercises. (See page 24.) It is easier to polish all three heart designs at the same time.

Crafter's notes

• The reason for placing the pewter onto a single layer of felt is to allow the pewter to indent as you are tracing. The softness of the felt provides the "give" that the metal needs in order to be molded.
• You will find the correct pressure while working through the beginner's exercises. Some people will have to hold back; others will have to press much harder.

• If you want a thicker design line, retrace the design after removing the tracing paper, using a medium-size ball tool. This will widen the line.
• Should you struggle initially with working out the right and wrong side of the pewter, mark the back with a permanent marker (press lightly) so you don't get confused.
• If you are heavy handed, you might find it easier to place the pewter onto a self-healing cutting mat or mouse pad instead of the felt, as they are slightly harder and give more support. When doing handwriting in indented low-relief, I always use a cutting mat.

Heart 2 (raised low-relief)

This is done in almost the same way as indented low-relief. The main difference is you will trace the design on the back (or wrong side) of the pewter, which results in the design being slightly raised. This is not high relief; the design does not have to be filled with beeswax, as it is not high enough. I used this technique on the glass bowl with the colored-square design on page 92.

You will need

soft pencil (6B)
tracing paper
piece of pewter 2¾" x 2¾" (7 cm x 7 cm)
1 piece of felt
hard board
masking tape
tracer tool or small ball tool
lubricant
paper pencil
materials for polishing

1. Trace the heart design from page 127. Place a single layer of felt onto the hard board and then put the pewter, **wrong**-side up, on top of the felt. Secure well with masking tape.

2. Place tracing-paper design onto the pewter. Center the design and secure on all four sides with masking tape.

3. Using the tracer tool or small ball tool, trace the entire design onto the pewter — remembering to use lubricant.

4. Remove tracing paper and all masking tape. Rub over the pewter with your finger to flatten it.

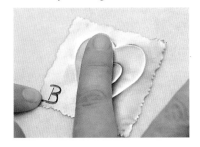

5. The design is now indented into the pewter. If you are light handed, you may need to retrace the design, pressing harder this time — do this without the tracing paper. If you are happy with the depth of the design, do not retrace.

6. Turn pewter over (right-side up) and place onto the hard board. Using the paper pencil, "draw" on

each side of the raised design lines in order to flatten those areas. Repeat this step on the inside heart.
7. Polish the pewter. (See details on page 24.)

Crafter's notes

• Retrace the heart onto a fresh piece of tracing paper each time you need to use it. The tracer tool scores the tracing paper as you trace, so the second time you use the tracing paper it may tear, causing you to lift your tool and thereby create broken lines.

• With raised low-relief the design will be in mirror image on the front. This is important to remember when doing numbers or letters of the alphabet — they need to be done in reverse on the back of the pewter.

High relief

This is where we start to do a little bit of sculpturing, so things get more exciting. For high relief, we model the design out from the back of the pewter in order to create the raised image on the front. The indentations in the back are then filled with beeswax or crack filler to support the design and prevent it from being pressed flat. When sculpturing your design, remember to concentrate on the shape of the design, rather than trying to model the pewter out as far as it can go. The secret to a good final shape is to model the design out very slowly.

Heart 3

High relief is a step-by-step process, so use the following steps whenever you are doing high relief — the process doesn't change. If you're new to this craft, you may have to refer back to these steps a couple of times when moving on to other projects in the book. However, before long you'll have the hang of it, and the process will come naturally.

You will need

soft pencil (6B)
tracing paper
piece of pewter 2³⁄₄" x 2³⁄₄" (7 cm x 7 cm)
hard board
masking tape
tracer tool or small ball tool
lubricant
3 pieces of felt

teaspoon
paper pencil
hockey-stick tool
beeswax
glass dropper
turpentine
cotton wool
patina
materials for polishing (see page 24)

1. Trace the heart design from page 127. Place pewter, right-side up, onto the hard board (not the felt). Secure the pewter and tracing paper well with masking tape. Trace the whole design using your tracer tool. Press harder than if you were writing.

2. Remove all masking tape. Flatten with your finger. Turn pewter over (wrong-side up). Spread a small amount of lubricant onto the back of the pewter.

3. Place the pewter onto a double layer of felt. Using the back of the teaspoon, start modeling the large heart. Keep the spoon flat — do not allow the edge of the spoon to touch the pewter. Work the spoon in small circles inside the design lines of the large heart, as if you are coloring it in. At this stage ignore the small inside heart — model over it as if it is not there. (Note: Do not press hard or model the shape out too far. If you do, the pewter will buckle when you try to neaten up in step 4. Once the pewter is stretched too far, the process cannot be reversed. This is the time to be very light handed.)

4. Turn the pewter over and place it onto the hard board. Using the paper pencil, trace around the large heart. Stay on the design line. You will notice this step turns the "bump" into a definite heart shape — it neatens up and defines the design. (Note: You should still be ignoring the small inside heart.)

5. Repeat steps 3 and 4 as many times as it takes to mold the large heart to the height you require. It will probably be three to four times. (Note: Remember to neaten up on the hard board, and to take the pewter out just a little in step 3.)

6. Once the large heart is the height you require, place the pewter wrong-side up on two layers of felt. Using the hockey stick, mold out the small inner heart. You may need to go onto a third layer of felt (see crafter's notes). Continue to mold the inner heart until it is the height you desire. (Note: Do not hold the hockey stick

like a pen, as this places the tool onto its pointy nose, which will create grooves. Make sure the tool is flat so you are able to work with the heel of the tool.)

7. Once this step is complete, place design right-side up onto the hard board, and neaten up with the paper pencil by drawing around the outside of the large heart. Pay no attention to the inner heart. For the final neatening up, use the tracer tool instead of the paper pencil to "draw" around the outside line of the large heart. Take care to stay on the design line, otherwise a second design line will be created. You will notice how this gives the design line definition.

8. Fill the back of the design with beeswax, using the glass dropper. Allow to harden.

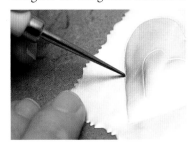

9. Place design, wrong-side up, onto a single layer of felt. This prevents it from getting scratched.

Clean off any excess wax with turpentine on cotton wool, using a new piece of cotton wool once the one you're working with is full of wax. (*Note: The wax must be level with the edge of the design. No wax should be outside of the design, as this will mold onto the front during the polishing process. If the wax solidifies in the dropper, it is not hot enough.*)

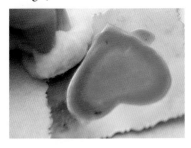

10. Turn the pewter over, right-side up, and place onto the hard board. Define the small inner heart by using the tracer tool to "draw" around it. Stay on the design line.

11. Patinate and polish the pewter. (See page 24.)

Crafter's notes

• In step 1, the pewter was placed onto the hard board as we only wanted to transfer the design to the pewter — we didn't want to start modeling the design. By tracing on the hard board, we create a deep scratch, not any form of relief.

• In step 4, the pewter was placed onto the hard board to neaten up around the design. If this is done on the soft cloth the design line will be indented, creating a trough around the design.

• The design is placed on two layers of felt while modeling, as this creates a soft surface that the pewter can mold into. We only ever start with two layers of felt, adding an extra layer as needed — this prevents the pewter from buckling into a surface that is too soft.

• Once you have worked through the softness of the two layers of felt, you need to add a third layer. This will happen when the design has been raised quite high, and, when trying to mold out further, the top surface of your shape is flat rather than rounded.

• The inside heart of this design represents the second level of any design. For example, the eye and gills of the fish on the sushi plate (see page 100).

• You don't have to clean off the lubricant from the back of the pewter before filling it with beeswax. However, if you are using any other form of filler, you will need to clean it off first.

Polishing process

The polishing process is the final step. This is done to antique and add depth to the pewter. The patina and polish will sit darkest in the indented areas of the design, giving the design depth. For this reason, all relief work and all final indented designs must be done before polishing, as they will not show up if done afterward. I must add, at this point, that I spend more time teaching people how to polish with metal polish, than how to work with pewter, but with a little practice you will get it right.

You will need
hard board
cotton wool
turpentine
tissues
degreaser (baby powder)
rubber or latex gloves
patina
household metal polish

1. Place the completed pewter design right-side up onto the hard board. Clean the front of the pewter with a piece of cotton wool and turpentine. Wipe clean with a tissue. Dip a piece of cotton wool into the baby powder and rub gently over the front of the design to remove all grease. *(Note: The patina will not take where there is grease.)*

2. Wearing the gloves, absorb patina onto a small piece of cotton wool and apply evenly over the entire piece of pewter. Rinse off in clean water to neutralize the effect of the patina. Pat dry with a tissue. *(Note: The metal will become very dark as you apply the patina but it will lighten once polished.)*

3. Place the pewter, right-side up, onto the hard board. Absorb a little metal polish onto a piece of cotton wool and rub over the pewter. Buff off gently with a clean piece of cotton wool. Replace the cotton wool once the piece you are using becomes black. *(Note: It is almost impossible to buff off dry metal polish without going through the tin layer of the pewter. Always remove dry polish with wet polish. Rub a little polish on a small area, then buff until shiny. Once the polish dries, apply a little more wet polish and buff. Move onto the next small area and work the same way. Don't rub hard or you will go through the top tin layer, exposing the layer underneath.)*

Crafter's notes

• The patina does not protect the metal in any way. It is done purely for aesthetics. If you want to leave the pewter in its shiny state, you do not have to apply patina or polish. You can just degrease to clean up the front of the pewter design.

• You can apply patina more than once, but the pewter will become extremely dark after the second application.

• The longer the patina is left on the pewter, the darker it will become — rinse it off straight away, or leave it on for up to 20 minutes. Experiment with different times to see the effects. You can dilute the patina with water to lessen the effect.

• Don't rub hard when applying the patina, or when polishing, as you may rub through the shiny tin layer.

• If you want the indented areas to be darker, try polishing with black stove polish. This polish does not remove the patina, so use after you have shined up the pewter with the metal polish.

• Do not get patina on metal tools — it will cause them to rust. If you do spill some on the tools, rinse in clean water.

Sculpturing

I have taken you through the low-relief and high-relief techniques. Once you understand them, you will be able to create almost any design. However, you need to understand how to sculpture, or work in various heights, when doing high relief. I have also done indented low-relief on the designs, so that we can work through combining the two techniques. These designs have been chosen for learning technique, rather than for the designs themselves. I will take you step by step through the ice cream, which is cut out. You can then practice the techniques you have learned to create the acorn — both designs are very similar. I used a pair of deckle-edge scissors to create the interesting border around the acorn and the green card. I have numbered the various height levels on the designs, with number 1 being the lowest level.

ICE CREAM

You will need

soft pencil (6B)

tracing paper

piece of pewter 4" x 2 $\frac{1}{2}$" (10 cm x 6 cm)

self-healing cutting mat or mouse pad

masking tape

tracer tool or small ball tool

lubricant

4 pieces of felt

teaspoon

hockey-stick tool

hard board

paper pencil

beeswax

glass dropper

turpentine

cotton wool

patina

materials for polishing

nail scissors or craft knife

colored card

glue

1. Trace the ice-cream design on page 127 onto tracing paper. Place the pewter, right-side up, onto the cutting mat or mouse pad. Secure pewter and tracing paper well with masking tape. Using the tracer tool, trace the design onto the pewter (see crafter's notes). Remove all masking tape.

2. Turn the pewter over, wrong-side up, onto two layers of felt. Using the teaspoon, mold out the

cone and ice cream, then use the hockey stick to mold out the cherry — and don't forget to use lubricant. Take all three sections out to the same height. Work these sections separately, and do not mold over the design lines that separate them.

3. Turn the pewter over, right-

side up, and place it onto the hard board. Using the paper pencil, "draw" around the outside of the design to neaten up the "bump." Do not define any lines on the inside of the design. (*Note: Remember to model the design out slowly, otherwise it will buckle when neatening up on the hard board.*)

4. Repeat steps 2 and 3 until all three sections of the design are the same height as you require the cherry to be — this is level 1.

5. Place the pewter, wrong-side up, onto two layers of felt. Mold out the cone and ice-cream sections to the required height for the

cone — this is level 2. (*Note: Do not model the cherry, as it is level 1, and you have already completed that level.*)

6. Turn the pewter over, right-side up, place it onto the hard board and, using the paper pencil, draw around the outside of the entire design. You have now completed level 2.

7. Place pewter, wrong-side up, onto three layers of felt. Mold out only the ice-cream section — this is level 3. (*Note: A dollop of ice cream will have a bumpy form, so use your artistic flair and model the ice-cream section in an interesting shape.*) Turn the pewter over, place it onto the hard board, and, using the paper pencil, draw around the entire design. For final neatening up, use the tracer tool to draw around the design.

8. Fill the back with melted wax, using the glass dropper. Allow to harden. Clean off excess wax with turpentine on a piece of cotton wool.

9. Using the tracer, define the line beneath the cherry and then define the line that separates the ice cream from the cone. The criss cross lines on the cone should be deep enough, but if not, redefine them with the tracer.

10. Patinate and polish.

11. Cut out the design with a small pair of nail scissors or use a craft knife and cutting mat. The curve of the nail scissors must face away from the pewter design.

12. Glue the pewter ice-cream

design onto the colored card.

Crafter's notes

• For step 1, you can place the pewter onto hard board when tracing the design onto the pewter, and then redefine the lines on the ice-cream cone once the wax is inside. It is very tricky, although not impossible, to stay on the lines once the wax is in, as the cone shape creates a hill — and on this design there are lots of lines. By placing the pewter onto a cutting mat when tracing on the design, the traced design lines will be slightly deeper on the pewter, as the cutting mat is firm (but a little softer than the hard board), which means the lines on the cone will not have to be redefined.

• If you are light handed and are working in high relief, you may find it easier to use the cutting mat or mouse pad (instead of hard board) when transferring your designs from the tracing paper to the pewter, as this will help you to get a stronger design line.

• What you have done here is model your entire design to level 1, then on to level 2, and finally to level 3. All pewter relief modeling should be completed this way. It doesn't work to push out the highest level first, as this will become flattened when you then work on the lower levels. Use the numbering system on your tracing paper if it helps you. It is a very good way to plan your design.

Projects

You will be able to do all the following projects using the techniques that you have learned. I have listed the items and tools needed for each project, so that you know what you need in order to complete it. However, some of these items may not appear in the steps because we have already covered this set of instructions. I've chosen to lay the projects out in this way to avoid being repetitive (and end up with instructions that spread over two pages!). If you've worked with pewter before, or have completed the previous projects, you'll know what to do. If not, simply go back to the previous projects, select the one that refers to the technique needed, and use that as a guide.

Spiral-bound book

African design

For this project I have used both black and copper patina to create the different color tones on the pewter. I applied the copper patina to the chosen areas using a watercolor paintbrush. The chemical reaction of the copper patina on the pewter creates a very different look and feel to the oxidizing effect of the black patina. Being the great scientist that I am, I cannot tell you what the scientific chemical reaction *is*, but I *can* tell you that it is fabulous to experiment with, as you can create interesting designs and textures when using it. So once again, go forth, have fun and experiment.

PEWTER DESIGN

You will need

soft pencil (6B)
tracing paper
piece of pewter 5⅛″ x 3⅜″ (3 cm x
   8.5 cm)
hard board
masking tape
1 piece of felt
medium ball tool
tracer tool
lubricant
paper pencil
cotton wool
patina
materials for polishing
copper patina
pointed, soft watercolor paintbrush
tissue
fine permanent marker
   (size 4x0 or 0.007″ tip)

1. Trace the design from page 128 onto tracing paper. Place the pewter, wrong-side up, onto a single piece of felt. Trace all the raised, high-relief areas using the medium-size ball tool. These are all the straight line borders, the center spiral and the S-shaped designs. Complete these designs as for raised high-relief.

2. Place pewter, right-side up, onto a single layer of felt. Using the tracer tool, complete the rest of the design in indented low-relief. This covers the zigzag triangles, the corner spirals and the dots. You may be more comfortable replacing the tracing paper and tracing these designs onto the pewter, or you may want to do them

freehand (see crafter's notes).

3. Apply the black patina and then polish.

4. Dip the paintbrush into the copper patina, holding the brush against the side of the bottle to allow the excess patina to run back into the bottle. Brush the patina onto one of the triangles, using the tip of the brush. It takes a few backward and forward movements of the brush before the

copper color starts to show. Once you notice that the movement of the brush is no longer turning the metal copper, redip the brush into the patina and repeat the process.

Dab off any excess patina with a tissue.

5. Repeat step 4 on all the areas that need to be copper. When applying copper patina to the four little spirals in the corners, you will find that they lose the black color that defines them. As they are very fine spirals it is difficult to "paint" around them. Once you have completed the copper-patina process, use the black permanent marker to "redraw" the black into the spirals.

(I think this is cheating a bit, but we won't tell.) The large center spiral is large enough to be "painted" around with the paintbrush.

6. Once you have finished coloring all the required areas with the copper patina, rinse the pewter under the tap. Pat dry with a tissue.

Crafter's notes
• African designs are more rhythmic than mathematical, so the designs do not have to be all the same size and shape. Feel free to do the designs freehand.
• Not all craft stores stock copper patina, but you will find it at a stained- glass studio or store.

THE BOOK

You will need
3 pieces of colored paper
   (eg., orange, brown and green)
ruler
pencil
craft knife and cutting mat
glue
2 pieces of firm, thin black cardboard, 5.8" x 8.3" (148 mm x 210 mm) size
white 5.8" x 8.3" (148 mm x 210 mm) size paper (number of pages depends on the book's thickness)

1. Cut the orange paper $4^3/_4$" x $6^{11}/_{16}$" (12 cm x 17 cm), the brown paper $4^5/_{16}$" x $6^1/_8$" (11 cm x 15.5 cm) and the green paper $3^3/_4$" x $5^1/_2$" (9.5 cm x 14 cm). Glue the brown paper onto the orange paper, and the green paper onto the brown paper. Make sure they are centered correctly.

2. Cut a $3^1/_8$" x $4^{15}/_{16}$" (8 cm x 12.5 cm) rectangle from the center of the paper frame. (*Note: You will cut through all three layers of paper.*)

3. Glue the pewter design in the center of one of the pieces of black cardboard. Glue the frame over the pewter. Place under a heavy book for about 1 hour until the glue has set.

4. To complete the book, lay down the plain black cardboard, place the pile of white paper on top, and the pewter-adorned cover on top of that. Have the book spiral bound with silver wire binding (see crafter's notes).

Crafter's notes
• Most stationery and photocopy stores will guillotine the paper to the size you require for a nominal fee. Most of them also do the binding. Ask for silver wire binding.
• There are two ways to mount the pewter onto the cover: you can use the colored paper as a frame, which is placed over the edges of the pewter, or you can glue the pewter on top of the background papers. The first way is slightly more difficult but gives a better finish; it also protects the corners of the pewter, so they don't lift with lots of wear and tear.

Flopsy

I have a studio cat. Her name is Flopsy. She lives in the house next door to my studio. She can be as vicious as she can be sweet and loving. Most mornings when I come to work, Flopsy is waiting for me at the door and greets me with a loud meow when I arrive. I still haven't worked out if I am in trouble for keeping her waiting or if she is really happy to see me. Either way, my coming to work is important to her. As soon as I sit down, she decides that the chair I have chosen is the one *she* wants, and if I try to move her, she attacks me by biting and scratching — hard. (She always wins.) Then she purrs lovingly and looks at me with an expression that lets me know how much I mean to her.

From then on she keeps me company. When it is time to leave the studio, she goes back into attack mode. I tip her off the chair so that I can put her outside — she then attacks my feet, spits, hisses and swears at me in three official languages. In fact, I often work longer just because I do not have the courage to put Flopsy out! So in her own strange way, she is one of the reasons I get all my work done …

One afternoon she was sitting on the windowsill, looking out and just basking in the warm sunlight. She looked so sweet and serene that I decided to draw her.

This design (on page 128) is completed in high relief. Once the wax is in, use the tracer to "scratch" on the fur. Complete the whiskers in indented low-relief. Using the black patina, patinate and polish the whole design.

Use a soft, watercolor paintbrush to brush on the copper patina around the cat. (See Spiral-bound book, page 31.) Dab off any excess patina with a tissue. Rinse in water and pat dry with a tissue.

To create the textured background, polish again with the metal polish. It will remove some of the copper patina as you polish, thereby creating the textured look.

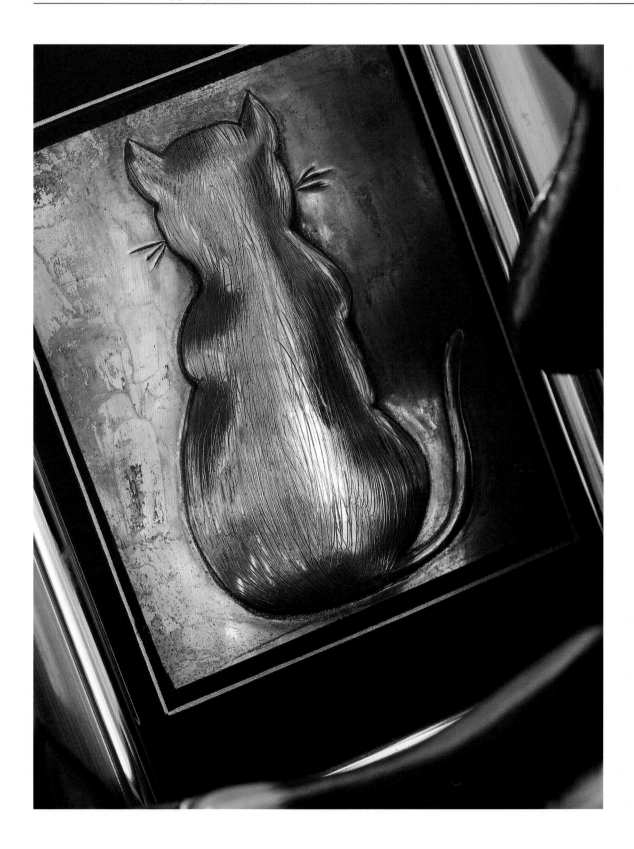

Treasure-box book-tin

This is a special gift to you. A place for you to safely tuck all those thoughts, ideas and designs that one day, when life hands you a bit of time, you will turn into beautiful crafts. The treasure box holds a beautiful, handcrafted leather-bound book, which hides in its pages a leather-and-pewter bookmark. The words on my tin are:

"In the centre of your heart,
is a small part,
And that is where your soul
must go to dream."

Julia Cameron

The pewter design on the tin is completed in both high and low relief. This is a good project for putting all your techniques together.

THE TIN (PEWTER LID)

You will need

tin or box (this one measures
    8¼" x 5½" or 21 cm x 14 cm)
soft pencil (6B)
tracing paper
pewter
hard board
3 pieces of felt
masking tape
tracer tool or small ball tool
lubricant
hockey-stick tool
teaspoon

paper pencil
beeswax and glass dropper
turpentine
cotton wool
craft knife and cutting mat
patina
materials for polishing
black stove polish
glue
glass paints
acetone
small, pointed, soft paintbrush

1. Cut a piece of tracing paper to fit the lid of the tin. Trace the design from page 129 onto this paper. Place the pewter right-side up onto hard board, and trace the design onto the pewter (see crafter's notes).

2. Complete the woman, the outer section of the "plant" and the outer circle of the bottom design in high relief. When modeling the woman, take the body, together with the arms and legs, out very

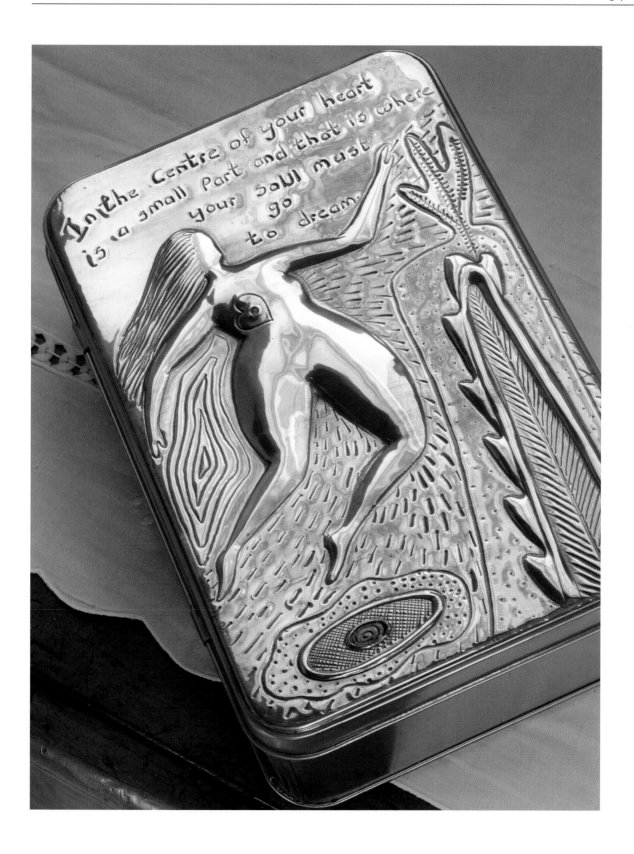

slowly. The arms and lower legs are much narrower than the rest of the body, so they will not be able to stretch out as far. Here you will have to take care: if the main section of the body is modeled too high, the areas where it meets the narrow limbs will buckle. You will notice that where the hair starts on the head the design is raised, whereas the end of the hair is flat. You need to create a gentle gradient from the head to the end of the hair in order to avoid creating a line where the head ends.

3. Once all the high relief has been done, turn the pewter, wrong-side up, onto a single layer of felt. Using the tracer, "draw" the circle in the center of the heart. (*Note: Do not define from the right side until the wax is in.*) Complete the inner circle of the bottom design in raised low-relief.

4. Place the pewter, right-side up, onto the felt and complete all indented low-relief, except for the handwritten poem.

5. Fill with wax and clean off excess with turpentine.

6. Place the pewter, right-side up, onto a cutting mat, and, using the tracer or small ball tool, write the words of the poem. (*Note: As the design has been filled with wax, you can comfortably rest your wrist on the design while writing, without flattening the design.*) Using the ball tool, create an indentation inside the circle on the heart — this needs to be indented to hold the glass paint.

7. Patinate and polish. (*Note: I polished the design with stove polish after I had finished polishing with the metal polish, in order to create more black in the indented areas of the design.*)

8. Glue the pewter design onto the lid. Allow the glue to set, and then trim off excess pewter by running the craft knife around the lid. Run the paper pencil around the edges of the pewter in order to mold the edges to the tin.

9. Dip the paintbrush into the glass paint; fill in the small circle on the heart, and also the circle on the bottom design. Clean the brush off in acetone, and then wash it with soap and water.

Crafter's notes

• You might find it easier to do some of the indented low-relief designs freehand, rather than tracing them. Examples would be the dots, the cross-hatching between the circles and the veins of the plant. It is definitely easier to write freehand than to trace handwriting.

• When tracing the design from the tracing paper onto the pewter, I masked the pewter onto a self-healing cutting mat instead of hard board. This gave the design lines a little more indentation than hard board will allow, which meant I didn't have to retrace any of the indented low-relief. I then did all my freehand indented low-relief on the cutting mat as well, so all the low relief would have the same depth. So, experiment!

THE LEATHER BOOK

You will need

paper for pattern

1 piece of soft leather (see crafter's notes)

pencil or chalk

craft knife or pair of scissors

1 button

sharp, pointed tool or thick, pointed needle for piercing leather

waxed thread or any thin, strong thread or string

darning needle

20 pieces of paper, cut to size

small piece of pewter

all materials to complete high-relief design

materials for polishing

glue

glass paint

small, pointed, soft paintbrush

acetone

1. Work out the size of your book, according to the size of your tin or box. Make a paper pattern for the size and shape of the leather cover (see crafter's notes). Draw this pattern onto the inside of the leather. If the leather is light in color, use a pencil; if it is dark, use white chalk. Using a craft knife or sharp pair of scissors, cut out the leather cover.

2. Fold the leather into the shape of the book and run your fingers down the folds to create the creases.

3. Work out where the button should be positioned, and pierce two holes, approximately $\frac{1}{8}$" (3 mm) apart, for the button.

Thread the darning needle with the wax thread, push the needle through the hole in the leather (from the back of the cover through to the front of the cover), and leave a length of wax thread. Thread the button onto the needle and push the needle through the second hole in the leather, returning to the back of the cover.

4. Remove the needle from the wax thread and tie the two ends of thread together to secure the button in place.

5. Mark and then pierce the two holes for the looped-thread button fastener — the holes should also be about $\frac{1}{8}$" (3 mm) apart. Use the

darning needle to thread the wax thread through the leather. Make sure the loose ends of your thread are on the outside of the cover. Tie all four ends together to create the thread button fastener. (*Note: I used a double thread for the button fastener.*)

6. On the crease of the leather, which will become the spine of the book, mark the holes for the thread that will sew the pages to the cover. (*Note: My book is 7", or 18 cm, in height and my holes are $1\frac{3}{16}$", or 3 cm, from the edges of the cover.*)

7. Using the sharp, pointed tool or needle, pierce the holes through the leather. Fold the pile of paper in half to create the pages of the book. Pierce holes, to correspond with the holes in the leather cover, through the folded pages (see crafter's notes).

8. To sew the pages to the cover, thread the darning needle with

the wax thread. Pass the needle through the bottom hole in the leather cover, from the back to the front, then through the top hole in the cover (from the front to the back), taking it through the

top holes of the pages. Now bring the thread down along the inside fold of the pages, finally taking it through the bottom holes in the pages. Tie a knot where the two threads meet at the bottom of the book, between the pages and the leather cover. Well done! You are now not only a master pewterer, but a bookbinder as well.

9. Cut an oval of pewter and complete the heart design on page 128 in high relief. Once the heart is completed, place the pewter, wrong-side up, onto a single piece of felt, and use the tracer tool to trace the outline of the center circle. Fill with wax, and when dry, use the tracer to define the circle.

10. Patinate and polish. Glue in place onto the leather cover. Place a drop of glass paint into the indentation and leave to dry. Clean the paintbrush with acetone, followed by soap and water.

Crafter's notes

• The piece of leather should be large enough to cover both sides of the book and make a flap on the front of the book. I used a large soup bowl as a template to create the semicircle shape of the flap on the front.

• Most stationery or art stores that supply paper will cut paper to size — ask when buying the paper. The paper should be cut at least 3/16" (5 mm) smaller on all sides than the cover; this prevents the paper protruding from the sides.

• When marking the holes on the pages, use one page as a pattern. Tape that page into position on the inside leather cover. Turn the cover over, push the needle through the holes in the leather, and you will pierce the page. Remove the masking tape and place this marked page on top of the rest of the pile of pages. Now pass the sharp tool through these holes (and through the rest of the pages).

THE BOOKMARK

You will need

1 piece of leather, 1" (2.5 cm) x the length of your tin
craft knife and cutting mat
metal ruler
piece of pewter
materials for completing indented low-relief
patina
materials for polishing
glue

1. Using the craft knife, cutting mat and metal ruler, cut the fringe of the bookmark. (*Note: The fringe should start about 3/16" (5 mm) below the pewter design — see crafter's notes.*)

2. Place pewter, right-side up, onto a single layer of felt. Complete the design on page 129 as for indented low-relief.

3. Patinate and polish. Adhere in place on the bookmark.

Crafter's notes

• Mark the straight line from where the fringe will be cut with a piece of masking tape. Each tassel is approximately 1/8" (3 mm) wide. Mark these measurements onto the tape.

• These bookmarks use up your scraps of pewter and make great gifts.

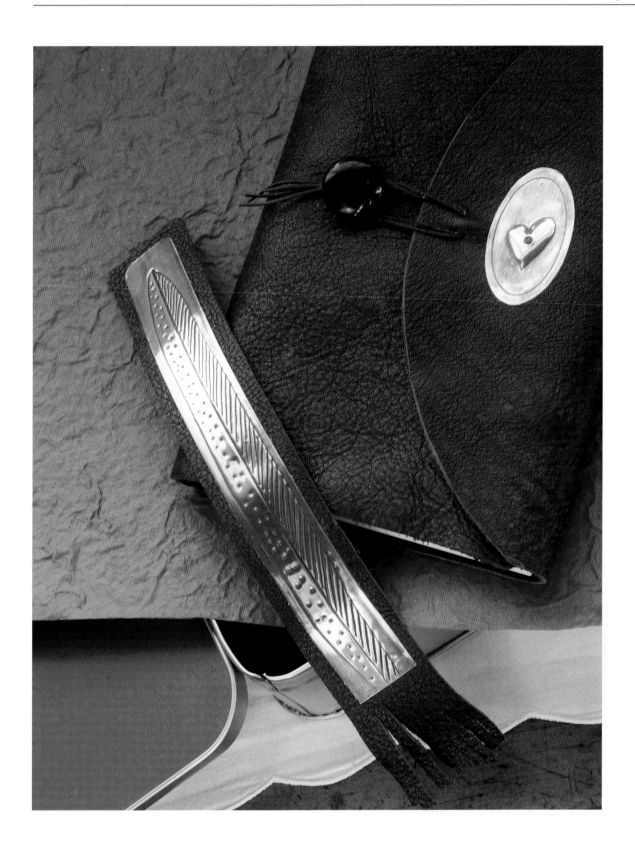

Decorative plaques

These are good examples of combining high relief with raised and indented low-relief in order to create interesting designs. Note how the black sits in the indented areas, and the raised areas remain silver. The indented low-relief helps to create the fine detail, like the veins on the leaves and the hairs on Samson's chest. The indented low-relief, which is done on top of the high relief, must be done after filling with beeswax, but *before* the patinating and polishing process. The reason for this is that the high-relief design needs to be supported while "drawing" on the low-relief detail. The indented details need to be created so they can hold the patina and polish.

You will need

soft pencil (6B)

tracing paper

piece of pewter 5$\frac{1}{8}$" x 5$\frac{1}{8}$" (13 cm x 13 cm)

hard board

masking tape

tracer tool or small ball tool

lubricant

3 pieces of felt

hockey-stick tool

medium-size ball tool (optional)

teaspoon

paper pencil

beeswax and glass dropper

turpentine

cotton wool

patina

materials for polishing

AFRICAN ANGEL

1. Trace the design from page 131. Place the pewter, right-side up, on hard board. Secure the pewter and tracing paper with masking tape and trace the entire design onto the pewter.

2. Mold out all the high-relief areas, following the steps for high relief. Use the hockey stick for the moon and face, the paper pencil for the star and the top of the hill, a teaspoon for the body and wings, and the medium-size ball tool to mold the hair strands. Keep the line between the body and the wings at surface level. Mold out the face just a little — it should not be as high as the body.

3. Once all high relief-steps are completed, place the design, wrong-side up, onto a single layer of felt. Using the tracer tool, very gently press out the nipples. Do not neaten up around them on the front of the design until the wax is in. Fill the design with beeswax and clean off any excess.

4. Place design, right-side up, onto a single layer of felt. Use the tracer tool to retrace all parts of the design that are indented low-relief. These are the sun, the designs on the wings, the breast line, the belly button, the line separating the legs, and the grass. Define the nipples with the paper pencil.

5. Patinate and polish.

SAMSON & DELILAH

Complete from the design on page 130 using the same techniques as for the African angel.

Crafter's notes
• Both of these designs will look stunning on the cover of a book.
• I had them both professionally framed and it's worth the extra expense. The red border around the designs adds lovely color.

Three red canvases

This project requires you to loosen up, hand over the controls and have fun. You will not be able to create canvases exactly the same as mine. If I had to repeat the process they would turn out very differently as they are abstract. You *will* have control over the pewter designs though.

I used fabric paint on the canvases because I have vast quantities of it in my studio — it is one of my other passions — but you can use any acrylic or craft paint. If you know how to work with oils, these will work too, and you won't have to apply varnish over the oil paints.

PEWTER PROJECT

You will need

soft pencil (6B)
tracing paper
pieces of pewter
1 piece of felt
hard board
masking tape
tracer tool or small ball tool
paper pencil
materials for polishing
Black stove polish
glue

1. Using the photo on page 45 as a guide, and the three small templates on pages 130-131, complete each design as for indented low-relief.

2. Patinate and polish. Leave the patina on for about 5 minutes, as you want the design to be dark. Once you have completed polishing with household metal polish, polish with the black stove polish to ensure the indented designs are as black as possible.

3. On the top-left and bottom-right canvases, glue the pewter pieces in place before painting. For the bottom-left canvas with the pewter border, we will glue the pewter border in place after the painting process is complete and the paint is dry. *(Note: The pewter border can be cut as one long strip or as four separate strips — separate strips are more economical. Measure the lengths you will need and add on at least 3/8" (10 mm) extra to allow for joins. Bear in mind that you can trim off excess pewter, but not add more. The pewter border overlaps the back of the canvas by 3/16" (5 mm) and the front by 3/8" (10 mm). Remember to add this to the measurement of the depth of your canvas. My canvases are 1 3/8" (35 mm) deep, so the width of my strips is 1 15/16" (50 mm).)*

CANVAS PAINTING

You will need

3 canvases 6" x 6" or 15 cm x 15 cm
  (or any size you prefer)
old plate
small container of premixed crack
  filler
wood glue
blunt knife
soft, flat paintbrush
water-based paint: red, brown, black
  and gold (or colors of your choice)
high-gloss, water-based varnish

1. Place about 3 tablespoons of premixed crack filler onto the plate and mix about ½ teaspoon of wood glue into the crack filler.
2. Using the blunt knife, place the crack filler onto the canvas. Build the crack-filler borders up around the pewter pieces. On the first canvas, I placed a border around the pewter and also built up a border on two opposite corners. I smoothed the outside edge of the pewter border onto the canvas using a wet, soft, flat paintbrush. I didn't use filler on the rest of the canvas. On the second canvas, I once again created a raised border around the pewter but also

created texture on the canvas, using the filler and the paintbrush. For the third canvas, I added a

little more wood glue to the filler mix to create a more liquid mix. I spread it over the front of the canvas, then, using the wet paintbrush, I created a smoother texture than on canvas number two.
3. Leave to dry completely. It will take 24–48 hours. Drying time will depend on the weather and the thickness of the filler.
4. Using the same paintbrush, apply the paint to the canvases. As the fabric paints I used are translucent, I applied the lighter color first and the darker shades over this. I painted red over the canvas first, building up the darker shades with brown. I used a little black paint between the pewter and the crack-filler borders to give more depth to these areas. I then brushed a little gold paint onto the borders and various places on the canvas. Work on the front of the canvases first, and only once they are dry, paint the sides. The trick with painting is to just relax and go with it, standing back from the

canvas every now and then to give you perspective. Remember there is no right or wrong way, and once you are happy with the effect, it is finished. (*Note: Paint one canvas at a time, then move on to the next — the paint needs to be wet in order to blend.*)
5. Once the paint is completely dry, paint on two coats of varnish, allowing the first coat to dry before applying the second coat.
6. Once the varnish on your third canvas is dry, you can glue on the pewter border. When you fold the pewter over the front of the canvas, you will need to trim one corner so that the corners meet neatly (see photos on page 91).

Crafter's notes

• The proportion of glue to crack filler does not need to be accurate — this is merely a guide, as some brands are slightly stiffer than others. The more glue you add, the more liquid the crack filler becomes. The important thing to remember is that the filler must be able to hold its shape.
• The wood glue dries clear and flexible, which gives the crack filler flexibility. Therefore, it won't crack with the movement of the canvas. Only use premixed crack filler, as it does not contract when dry, unlike powdered filler, which does.

Angel icon

An angel, a bird and a love song, all surrounded by gorgeous colors to create a magical feeling. Definitely to be made for someone special who appreciates the fun side of life.

PEWTER PROJECT

You will need

soft pencil (6B)
tracing paper
piece of pewter
hard board
masking tape
tracer tool or small ball tool
lubricant
2 pieces of felt
hockey-stick tool
paper pencil
beeswax and glass dropper
cotton wool
turpentine
patina
materials for polishing
stove polish
craft knife and cutting mat
gold permanent marker
  (available from stationery stores)

1. Trace the design from page 127. Complete as for high relief. Once the wax is solidified, use the tracing tool to retrace the flowers on the angel's wings, the twirl at the bottom of her spine and the detail on the bird. The lines connecting the two music hearts are done in indented low-relief.

2. Patinate and polish — leave the patina on for at least 5 minutes to create blackness in the wing detail.

3. After polishing with the metal polish, do the same with the stove polish. This will deepen the black in the indented details.

4. Cut out the design. Look carefully at the photograph on page 49 to see how I have cut it out. Cut on the design line around the left wing, under the angel's bottom, across to her ankle and under her feet.

5. Use the gold marker to color her halo and the music notes. (Note: Instead of using the gold marker, you could use gold leaf or copper patina.)

Wax sticks

You will need two toothpicks for your wax-stick set. Dip the tip of one toothpick into melted beeswax and allow the wax to harden. Use the waxed tip to pick up and place a single bead, and use the second, clean, toothpick to ease the bead off the wax stick and into position.

CANVAS PAINTING AND BEADING

You will need

soft pencil (6B)

tracing paper

1 canvas 6" x 6" or 15 cm x 15 cm
(or any size you prefer)

water-based paint: turquoise, white,
brown, dark brown and gold
(or gold marker)

small container of premixed crack
filler

old plate

wood glue

blunt knife

flat, soft paintbrush

cloth

satin-finish, water-based varnish

seed beads: orange, turquoise and
lime green.

set of wax sticks (see previous page)

1. Trace the shape of the brown frame onto the canvas using a pencil (see crafter's notes).

2. Paint the entire front of the canvas turquoise; brush a little white paint on the turquoise section above the frame outline. Allow the paint to dry.

3. Place about 3 tablespoons of premixed crack filler onto the plate, and mix about ½ teaspoon of wood glue into the filler.

4. Using the blunt knife, apply the filler to the marked-out frame shape and smooth it using a wet paintbrush. Shape the top of the frame with the side of the knife, and wipe away any filler that is

outside the lines with a damp cloth. Make sure the bottom of the frame is flush with the bottom edge of the canvas.

5. Using the back of the paint-brush, make indentations down the left and right sides of the frame. Allow the crack filler to dry. This will take 24–48 hours, depending on the weather and the thickness of the filler.

6. Paint the frame with the brown paint, and create the darker areas using the dark brown paint. Use the dark brown paint for the sides of the canvas too. Paint gold into the indentations (or use a gold marker). Once the paint is dry, varnish the canvas — front and sides — with two coats of vanish. Allow the first coat to dry before applying the second coat.

7. Glue the pewter to the canvas, ensuring that it is in the center of the frame.

8. Place wood glue onto the area of the canvas where the green beads will go. Place the green beads onto the glued area. Make sure the beads are lying on their sides and that the holes in the beads are not showing. Repeat this process with the orange and turquoise beads. Use a toothpick to turn the beads onto their sides, and a wax stick to pick up and place individual beads (see previous page).

Crafter's notes

• Trace the design of the frame onto tracing paper. Turn the tracing paper over and retrace the frame on the back of the tracing paper using a soft pencil (6B). Place the tracing paper, right-side up, onto the canvas, and draw over the design line of the frame. The design will be transferred onto the canvas.

• You can speed up the drying process of the paint and vanish by using a hairdryer. Do not speed up the drying process of the crack filler this way — it must dry naturally or it will crack.

• If the filler cracks when dry, it means too much water has been applied when smoothing with the wet paintbrush. This is not necessarily a bad thing: you will notice some cracks on the frame of my design, and I think, in this case, it enhances the design.

Mehendi hand

Glass paints. What fun! Look how gorgeous they are. This is a fantastic way to bring color onto pewter. Have a look at the glass bowl on page 93 and the cow black board on page 89. Glass paints are interesting to use, as they are not applied in the same way as other paints. You need to create a "dam wall" and then allow the paint to flow in. So no previous painting experience required …

The reason they work so well on pewter is that they are made to adhere to nonabsorbent surfaces and the smooth, shiny surface of the metal reflects light back through the paints, bringing them to life. This design uses both low-relief techniques.

You will need

soft pencil (6B)
tracing paper
piece of pewter
1 piece of felt
hard board
masking tape
tracer tool
medium-size ball tool
lubricant
paper pencil
patina
materials for polishing
glass paints: purple, deep red, blue and green (or colors of your choice)
soft, pointed watercolor paintbrush
acetone (check instructions on paint bottle for solvent required; most use acetone)

1. Trace the design on page 132 onto tracing paper. Place the pewter, right-side up, onto hard board, and trace the entire design onto the pewter using the tracer tool.
2. Place the pewter, right-side up again, onto a single layer of felt, and retrace all the indented low-relief designs with the tracer tool. (Note: These are all the designs under the glass paints.)
3. Turn the pewter over and place, wrong-side up, onto a single layer of felt. Retrace all the raised low-relief designs, using the medium-size ball tool.
4. Place the design onto hard board, right-side up, and use the paper pencil to "draw" on each side of the raised design lines in order to flatten the areas around

them. Repeat steps 3 and 4 twice. It is the raised low-relief lines that create the "dam walls," so they need to be quite high.
5. Patinate and polish.
6. Dip the brush into the color of paint required and allow the paint to flow between the raised lines. The brush needs to be loaded with paint. Help the paint flow into all required areas by dragging the brush into these areas. Clean the brush regularly in the acetone, as the paint dries quickly and clogs the brush. Clean the paintbrush thoroughly in acetone before using a new color.
7. Allow to dry completely — the glass paints will be hard when dry.

Crafter's notes

• Glass paints (or glass stain, as some manufacturers call them) are available at art and craft stores and are normally used to create a stained-glass look on glass.

• If the glass paints are thick, dilute with acetone (or required solvent), as the thick paint does not flow well or allow the underlying design to be seen clearly. Experiment on a small piece of pewter until you get the feel of the paints. These experimental pieces can be used to make greeting cards.

• The instructions on my brand of glass paints suggest using a paintbrush or a glass dropper. I found the paintbrush both easier to use and clean.

Pewter patchwork

The inspiration for this project came from a picture of a beautiful patchwork quilt that hangs in the Australian National Gallery. The background of the quilt was a deep blue and the rest of the colors were gorgeous and jewel-like. I was so inspired by the design and colors that I decided to try "patchwork" on pewter, using glass paints for color. This is my experiment. Also have a look at the Art deco glass bowl on page 93: I used the same patchwork design to adorn the edge of a clear glass bowl. Follow the step-by-step instructions for the glass bowl in order to create this project.

Backgammon table

The leather and pewter mix on this gaming table conjures up images of cigar smoke and whiskey, and we have had hours of fun around this table. The project will also work on a wooden board, cut to size, which can then be placed on top of a table. Cut the board either to the size of your tabletop or to the standard size of the square game board. The diameter of my table is $19^{11}/_{16}$" (50 cm) and the size of my game board is 14" x 14" (35.5 cm x 35.5 cm). Look around for playing pieces that suit your backgammon table. Fortunately, I had pieces from an old set that worked perfectly, but if you can't get your hands on any, try flat buttons, beads or metal disks.

LEATHER AND TRIANGLE DESIGN

You will need

table (or board cut to size)
leather to fit the size of the tabletop
craft knife and cutting mat
contact adhesive
soft pencil (6B)
tracing paper
ruler
masking tape
gold leaf
gold-leaf adhesive
black craft paint
shellac varnish
black permanent marker

1. Cut the leather to size. (*Note: It is safer to cut the leather a little bigger than your tabletop, as you can trim to size with a craft knife once it is glued onto the table.*) Glue the leather to the tabletop using contact adhesive.

2. Trace the design from page 133 onto tracing paper. Turn the tracing paper over and retrace the design on the back of the tracing paper, using the soft pencil. Place the tracing paper, right-side up, onto the leather, and then draw over the design using a ruler and pencil. The design will be transferred onto the leather canvas.

3. Place gold leaf onto the triangles that are to be covered with the leaf. Ensure that the sequence of black and gold triangles is correct — check the photo. (See how to gold leaf on page 57.) I rubbed a little black craft paint onto the gold leaf in order to "antique" it, before painting on the shellac. Be sure to only apply shellac over the gold-leafed sections. (*Note: Apply masking tape around the edges of the triangles before painting on the gold-leaf adhesive — you do not want glue outside the lines. Mask again before rubbing on black craft paint and applying shellac.*)

4. Use the black permanent marker to color in the black triangles, and, using a ruler, draw black outline around the gold triangles.

PEWTER GAME BOARD AND TABLE EDGE

You will need

pewter
hard board
ruler
craft knife and cutting mat
soft pencil (6B)
tracing paper
tracer tool
masking tape
lubricant
2 pieces of felt
hockey-stick tool
paper pencil
beeswax and glass dropper
turpentine
cotton wool
patina
materials for polishing
contact adhesive

Frame

1. Cut a piece of pewter to the shape and size of the game board. (I have used one piece.) Keep the remnants for another project.
2. Place pewter, right-side up, on the hard board. Trace the small designs from page 133 and then transfer the design to the pewter, using a tracer tool. Complete the fleur-de-lis and the continuous dotted design in high relief. Complete the indented border lines in indented low-relief.
3. Patinate and polish.
4. Glue into place onto the leather tabletop. (*Note: I used contact adhesive, and masked tape around the edge of the area that needed glue to prevent it from spreading to the rest of the board. Before using the masking tape, make sure the shellac varnish is completely dry.*)

Table edge

1. Measure the depth of the table and add ³/₈" (1 cm) to this measurement, as you need ³/₁₆" (5 mm) overlap for both the top and the underside of the table. Measure the circumference of your table and divide the measurement by four — it is more economical to use four strips than one long strip. Cut the four strips of pewter to the correct size.
2. Place one strip, right-side up, onto a layer of felt. Complete the design in indented low-relief. I scored the inside of each dot with the tracer, so it will hold more black when polished. Repeat this step with all four strips.
3. Patinate and polish all four strips of pewter.
4. Glue the strips to the edges of the table. Fold the pewter over the top and bottom edges of the table and run the side of the tracer tool over the folded sections to flatten and smooth them. (*Note: I have joined the strips at the corners of the gaming board.*)

Crafter's notes

• The reason I chose to do the triangles on the board in gold and black, rather than using pewter, is because pewter triangles glued to the top of the leather will not be durable. The pointy tips will start to lift in time, and the buttons will not slide easily over the triangles when being moved during a game. However, a way to get around this is to cut triangles in the leather in to which the pewter can be placed.
• All the designs for this project (the black and gold triangles and the pewter designs) need to be sized to fit your tabletop or board. This can be done on a photocopier.
• Instead of using gold leaf, you can use a permanent gold marker. Varnish with water-based varnish for durability.
• Any excess glue can be cleaned off with turpentine.

HOW TO GOLD LEAF

True gold leaf is very expensive and not easily available. We use the far less expensive alternative, known as metal leaf. This is available at art and craft stores and is sold in book form. The fine, delicate papers of the metal leaf are placed between sheets of tissue paper, so when cutting the metal leaf, cut together with a piece of the tissue paper that protects it. Lightly dust your hands with powder while working with the metal leaf, as perspiration from your hands may cause oxidization.

You will need

shellac (blond): thin flakes of
    resinous substance used to make
    vanish
methylated spirits or white spirit
old stocking
small piece of cotton wool
small, inexpensive paintbrush
gold-leaf adhesive used for gilding
    (the term for "gold leafing")
talcum powder
sheets of gold leaf
small, sharp pair of scissors
acetone

1. Mix shellac flakes with methylated spirits or white spirit to form varnish — it should have the same consistency as normal wood varnish. (*Note: Mix up a lot more than needed and keep a screw-top bottle ready to fill — it can be kept for years, so you won't have to mix it every time you need it.*)

2. Cut a piece of stocking about 6¼" (16 cm) long, place a piece of cotton wool inside, and tie the stocking into a knot — this will be used as your "sandpaper."

3. Using the paintbrush and the gold-leaf adhesive, paint all areas you want to gild. Take care not to get glue on any areas that you do not want gilded.

4. Leave the adhesive to dry for about 15 minutes. It dries clear — do not place gold leaf over the adhesive if it is still milky, because it won't stick.

5. Powder your hands, cut out pieces of gold leaf and place them over the glue. Press down firmly. (*Note: You can overlap the pieces of gold leaf in order to cover the glued area. The pieces don't need to be cut to the exact size and shape of the area to be gilded.*)

6. Gently rub the stocking-covered cotton wool over you design. This will buff away all unwanted pieces of gold leaf, and leave the gilding smooth. Collect excess gold leaf and store for future use. Leave to dry for about an hour.

7. Paint the shellac over the gilded area, and, when finished, clean the paintbrush with acetone.

Crafter's notes

• If gold is not your color, shop around for silver or copper leaf. Some stores only stock the gold, but many do stock the other colors.
• Try polishing the gold leaf with stove polish before varnishing: this will give it an interesting antique look.
• The cotton-wool stocking tool also makes a great buffer.

Wedding album

A beautiful album to commemorate a special day. The silver of the pewter enhances the wedding theme. Why not offer to create a beautifully adorned pewter wedding album for a special friend as your wedding gift to her?

When adorning the pages of an album, let the photographs be the prominent feature. Use your pewter decorations to enhance, not detract from, the photographs. I like to work on the theory that less is more. One photograph per page may seem a bit extravagant, but it is very powerful.

Heart-shaped frame

Front cover

I cut out the pewter with a pair of deckle-edge scissors, which produces a pattern similar to the decorative borders of old photographs. Be sure to choose a photograph where the subject will fit nicely into the heart shape of the frame (see page 135).

You will need

large photograph
photo album
soft pencil (6B)
ruler
tracing paper
pewter
deckle-edge scissors
hard board
masking tape
tracer tool or small ball tool
lubricant
2 pieces of felt
medium-size ball tool
hockey-stick tool
paper pencil
beeswax
glass dropper
turpentine
cotton wool
craft knife and cutting mat
patina
materials for polishing
glue
35 flat back crystals (size ss12)
clear epoxy glue for beads
set of wax sticks (see crafter's notes)

1. Cut the pewter to size using the deckle-edge scissors. Place the pewter, right-side up, onto the hard board and trace the design on to the front of the pewter. Using the tracer tool, make dot marks where the crystals will be placed. Complete the heart, bells and rings as for high relief. Complete the indented outer border as for indented low-relief.

2. Fill the back with wax and clean off any excess. When the wax has set, cut out the center of the heart using the craft knife (see crafter's notes.) Patinate and polish the front of the pewter.

3. Glue the photograph in position on the front cover of the album, and then glue the pewter frame over the photograph.

4. Gently press the medium-size ball tool onto the dots on the heart frame to create a small indentation — this indentation will hold the glue beneath the crystal.

5. Glue crystals into position (I used the wax sticks with quick-set, clear epoxy glue.)

Crafter's notes

• Once you have traced the design from page 135 onto the tracing paper, place the tracing paper over the photograph you wish to use. Make sure that the heart frame does not cut off any important part of the subject in the photograph. If it does, adjust the shape of the heart or get the photograph resized.

• Always cut away areas of the pewter that are not going to be used for the project before applying patina and polishing, as these pieces may be used for other projects. Once they have been patinated, they will be wasted.

• You will need three toothpicks for your wax-stick set. Use one to place the glue into the indentation on the pewter. Dip the tip of the second toothpick into melted beeswax and allow the wax to harden: use the waxed tip to pick up and place a single crystal. The third, clean, toothpick can be used to ease the crystal into position on the glue.

Love frame

I have left the design on the top part of the frame simple, because the focus of this design is the word "LOVE" at the bottom of the frame.

You will need

large photograph

soft pencil (6B)

tracing paper

pewter

hard board

masking tape

tracer tool or small ball tool

lubricant

2 pieces of felt

paper pencil

beeswax and glass dropper

turpentine

cotton wool

craft knife and cutting mat

patina

materials for polishing

glue

1. Trace the designs from page 134 onto a piece of tracing paper. Place the pewter, right-side up, onto the hard board, and trace the design onto the pewter. Complete all the designs as for high relief. (A hockey-stick tool will be too large for the narrow letters and small designs on this frame, so use the paper pencil when modeling.)

2. Fill the back with beeswax and remove any excess using turpentine. Place the pewter, right-side up, onto the hard board. Retrace the details on the letters of the word LOVE, using the tracer tool.

3. Use the craft knife to cut out the center of the frame — keep the cutout for another project. Patinate and polish.

4. Glue the photograph into position and then glue the pewter frame over the photograph.

Crafter's notes

• When cutting out the inside to complete the frame, use a ruler to ensure that the sides are absolutely straight.

• Keep the cutout for other projects.

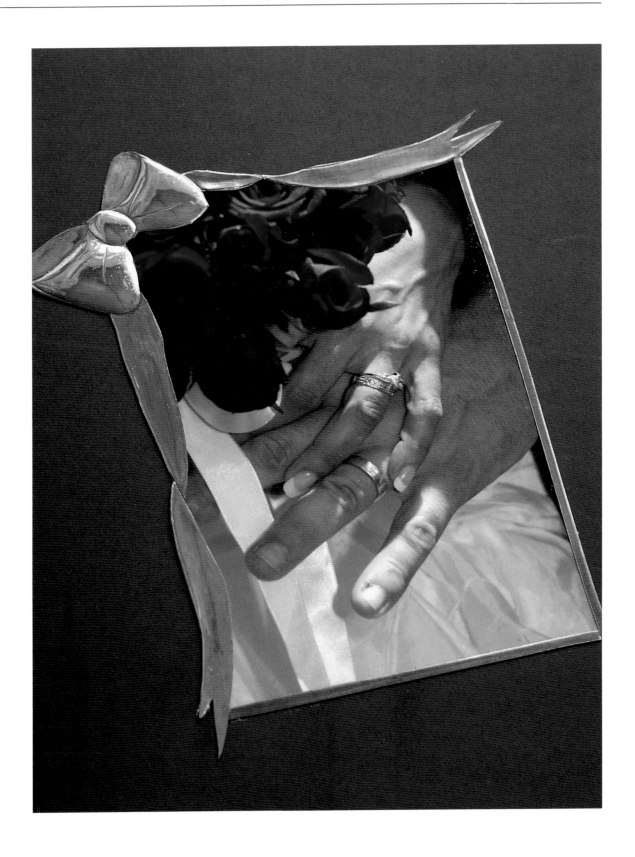

Silver ribbon frame

The inspiration for the ribbon design on this frame came from the picture itself — it works well with the ribbon on the bride's bouquet.

You will need

large photograph

soft pencil (6B)

tracing paper

pewter

hard board

masking tape

tracer tool or small ball tool

lubricant

2 pieces of felt

hockey-stick tool

paper pencil

beeswax and glass dropper

turpentine

cotton wool

patina

materials for polishing

copper patina

pointed watercolor paintbrush

tissue

glue

small pair of nail scissors or craft knife and cutting mat

1. Trace the ribbon design from page 134. Place the pewter, right-side up, onto the hard board. Trace the design onto the pewter. Complete the bow and the knot as for high relief. Leave the ribbons flat — do not mold them.

2. Fill the back of the bow with wax and remove the excess with turpentine. Using the tracer tool, retrace the indented design lines on the bow.

3. Apply the black patina and polish.

4. Dip the paintbrush into the copper patina and hold the brush against the side of the bottle to allow the excess patina to run back into the bottle. Brush the patina onto the top of the bow, using the tip of the brush. It takes a few backward and forward movements of the brush before the copper color starts to show. Once you notice that the movement of the brush is no longer turning the metal copper, redip the brush into

the patina and repeat the process. Dab off any excess patina with a tissue, rinse under the tap and pat dry with a tissue.

5. Cut out the pewter bow, using the pair of nail scissors. Have the curve of the blade facing away from the design when you cut. (You may find a craft knife and cutting mat easier to use.)

6. Glue the photograph into position, then place and glue the pewter bow into position over the photograph.

Crafter's note

• I have used two narrow pewter strips to frame the right-hand side and underneath the photograph. The strips have been patinated and polished. If your photograph has white borders, they will automatically frame these two sides of the photograph.

Long-stemmed rose

This single, feminine and elegant long-stemmed rose picks up the theme of the wedding perfectly. The design is completed as for high relief, and then cut out using a pair of small nail scissors. It has been positioned on the page so that it just cuts across the bottom corner of the photograph. The design is on page 132.

PEWTER LABEL

Small pewter frames make lovely labels. This one has been adorned with a simple, indented low-relief design. If you have a stylus tool and an oval stencil it will make the cutting out of the center oval much easier. Secure the pewter onto the cutting mat with masking tape, place the oval stencil in position over the pewter, and cut out using the stylus tool. The names have been written with a silver marker. The basic design is on page 132.

LARGE PEWTER FRAME

This large frame represents a free-standing photograph frame. I have placed a piece of textured paper behind the photograph. The deep red of the paper sets off the color of the roses. This is a lovely way to bring attention to a favorite photograph.

The pewter frame is $1\frac{3}{16}$" (3 cm) wide and the center frame (which is on the edge of the red paper) is $\frac{1}{16}$" (2 mm) wide. As it is more economical, I used four strips of pewter for each frame and joined them at 45-degree angles at the corners. The frames have been patinated and polished.

Bracelets

Make yourself some lovely antique silver bracelets: classic designs or bling-bling, the choice is yours. Gather together a selection of plastic or wooden bracelets and cover them with pewter. This is a good way to turn those old bracelets that you no longer wear into something new for yourself, or to create a special gift for someone else.

When choosing the bracelet, make sure that it is not too beveled. Bear in mind that pewter cannot be gathered, so the face of the bracelet should be quite flat. The bracelet with the crystals is about as beveled as you can go, without the pewter gathering when used for covering. The thickness or depth of the side of the bracelet does not matter. The two bracelets that I have used as a base for these two projects are different shapes, and therefore needed to be covered using slightly different techniques. Select a relevant technique based on the type of bracelet you will be using as your base.

Silver cross bracelet

This design has an African feel to it. The low-relief lines around the raised cross create a good contrast, as they hold the black patina, whereas the cross remains silver.

You will need

plastic or wooden bracelet
ruler
tracing paper
soft pencil (6B)
craft knife and cutting mat
pewter
hard board
masking tape
tracer tool
lubricant

2 pieces of felt
medium-size ball tool
paper pencil
beeswax and glass dropper
turpentine
cotton wool
patina
materials for polishing
glue

1. Measure the circumference of the bracelet and then the width, adding ⁵/₃₂" (4 mm) to the width (but not the circumference) measurement to allow for over-lapping. Cut a paper pattern from tracing paper to fit these measurements. Wrap the tracing-paper pattern around the bracelet to make sure it fits. Place the bracelet onto a piece of tracing paper, draw around the outer and inner circumference of the bracelet, and cut out to create a circular paper pattern. Place the pattern onto the bracelet to make sure it is the correct size. Cut your pewter to size using these patterns. (*Note: You will need to cut two strips of pewter: one to cover the inside and the other to cover the outside of the bracelet. You'll also have to cut two circles, for the top and bottom of the bracelet.*)

2. Trace the design from page 136 onto the relevant paper pattern.

3. Place the pewter, right-side up, onto the hard board, and secure with masking tape. Trace the high-relief designs onto the pewter. That is, the crosses and the horizontal border lines above and below the crosses. (*Note: It is easier to do the indented low-relief freehand.*) Complete these designs as for high relief. Fill the back with wax and clean off excess with turpentine.

4. Place the pewter, right-side up, onto a cutting mat. Use the tracer tool for the indented low-relief lines, taking the lines right up to the edge of the high-relief design.

5. Patinate and polish all four pieces of pewter.

6. Glue the strip of pewter that goes inside the bracelet into position. Fold the overlap of pewter over the edge of the bracelet, and run the side of the tracer along the edge to mold the pewter to it. Repeat this step with the pewter strip that goes on the outside of the bracelet. Ensure that the join on the outer strip is in the same position as the join on the inner one.

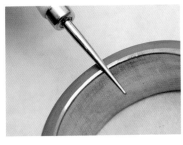

7. Glue a pewter circle to one side of the bracelet and press down

well. Run the edge of the tracer along the inner and outer edges of the pewter to mold the edges flat. Repeat with the remaining circle on the other side.

8. If using a mock clasp, glue it into position (see crafter's note).

Crafter's note
• To hide the pewter joins on the silver cross bracelet, create a mock clasp by cutting a ³/₁₆" (5 mm) wide strip of pewter that is long enough to fit around the bracelet like a clasp. I adorned the strip with a raised square to resemble part of a clasp. Patinate and polish the strip before gluing it in place.

Crafter's notes (page 69)
• The reason we place the pewter onto a cutting mat for step 4 of the crystal bracelet is to give the pewter more support, as the mat is not as soft as felt. If the pewter is placed onto a piece of felt, the indented dots will be too deep.
• To hide the pewter joins, I created a mock clasp by cutting a strip of pewter ³/₈" (1 cm) wide and long enough to fit around the bracelet like a clasp. I adorned the strip with an indented low-relief line on each side. Patinate and polish the strip before gluing in place.

Crystal bracelet

I have used clear crystals for the bracelet, though colored ones would also work well. If you prefer more color, try some of the deep, jewel-colored crystals.

You will need

plastic or wooden bracelet
ruler
tracing paper
soft pencil (6B)
craft knife and cutting mat
pewter
hard board
masking tape
tracer tool
lubricant
2 pieces of felt
medium-size ball tool
paper pencil
beeswax and glass dropper
turpentine
cotton wool
patina
materials for polishing
glue
90 flatback crystals (size ss5)
4 flatback crystals (size ss12)
clear epoxy glue
set of wax sticks (see page 59)

1. Measure the circumference of the bracelet and then the width, adding $5/32$" (4 mm) to the width (but not the circumference) measurement to allow for overlapping. Cut a paper pattern from tracing paper to fit these measurements.

Wrap the tracing-paper pattern around the bracelet to make sure it fits. Cut your pewter to size using this pattern. (*Note: You will need to cut two strips of pewter: one to cover the inside and the other to cover the outside of the bracelet.*)

2. Trace the design from page 136 onto the relevant paper pattern.

3. Place the pewter, right-side up, onto the hard board. Trace only the continuous curved line onto the pewter. Remove all masking tape.

4. Place pewter, right-side up, onto the cutting mat and reposition the tracing paper. (*Note: Make sure your pattern lines up.*) Using the tracer tool, make indented dots along the spiral pattern. Use a medium-size ball tool to indent the larger dots for the position of the large crystals.

5. Complete the continuous curved line as for high relief. When neatening up with the paper pencil, "draw" over each end of the line to "close off" the ends of the raised line – this prevents the wax from leaking out.

6. Patinate and polish both strips of pewter.

7. Glue the strip of pewter that goes inside the bracelet into position. Fold the overlap of pewter over the edge of the bracelet, and run the side of the tracer tool along the edge to mold the pewter to it. Repeat this step with the pewter strip that goes on the outside of the bracelet. Ensure that the join on the outer strip is in the same position as the join on the inner one.

8. This part is a little tricky on a bevel-faced bracelet: you will find that the edges gather a little. Work the gathers down with the side of the paper pencil, being careful not to flatten your design. Keep running the side of the paper pencil gently over the gathers, and they will eventually flatten out. Place a piece of masking tape over the join to keep it in place, as the glue has not yet set.

9. If using a mock clasp, glue it into position (see crafter's notes on the previous page).

10. Glue the crystals into position using the wax sticks. (*Note: I used clear, quick-set epoxy glue for the crystals.*)

Silver dangle earrings

Big, bold and elegant with just a touch of bling-bling: these earrings may look like solid silver, but they are much lighter.

You will need

wooden or plastic earrings
tracing paper
soft pencil (6B)
craft knife and cutting mat
pewter
ruler
hard board
masking tape
tracer tool or small ball tool
lubricant
1 piece of felt
medium ball tool
paper pencil
glue
beeswax and glass dropper
turpentine
cotton wool
patina
materials for polishing
4 small crystals (size ss5)
2 flatback crystals (size ss12)
clear epoxy glue
set of wax sticks (see instructions
  on page 59)

1. Remove the findings (hooks, wires, etc.) from the earrings. Place one earring onto the tracing paper. Draw around the outside and inside to create a paper pattern. Add $\frac{1}{16}$" (2 mm) to the outer edge of the circle and the same to the inner edge — this is to allow the pewter to overlap the edges of the earrings. Trace the design from page 136 onto the earring pattern that you have just made. *(Note: If your crystals for the central design are a different size, adjust the size of the circle on that part of the design.)*
2. Cut four pieces of pewter using the paper pattern (back and front for two earrings). Measure the *outer* circumference and depth

of your earring and cut two strips of pewter according to this measurement. Now measure the *inner* circumference and depth of the earring and cut the pewter strips accordingly. *(Note: It is safer to cut paper patterns for the strips, then place them in position to check they are the correct size, before cutting the pewter.)*
3. Lay the pewter piece that is to be the front of the earring onto the hard board, right-side up. Place the traced design onto the pewter and complete as for high relief. Fill with wax and clean off excess with turpentine. Repeat, to complete the pewter design for the second earring.

4. Patinate and polish all eight pieces of pewter.

5. Glue the back of the earring in place and press down well. Fold down the overlapping edges, running the side of the tracer tool around the edge of the earring to flatten the pewter. You will be able to flatten the gathers of pewter.

6. Gently press the tracer tool through the hole at the front of the disk, just hard enough to make a raised bump on the back of the pewter, so as to indicate the position of the hole for the finding. Using the "bump" as a guide, press the tracer through from the back of the disk to re-create the hole.

7. Repeat step 5 to glue the front of the earring in place.

8. Glue the back of the long strip of pewter into position. Make sure the join is at the top of the earring — it will be hidden under the jump ring. Press down well,

and run the side of the tracer tool around the edge of the earring to mold the strip into place. Repeat this procedure with the inner circle, once again ensuring that the join is at the top of the earring.

9. To locate the hole on the front of the earring, gently press the tracer tool through the hole from the back to create a bump. Using this mark as a guide, press the tracer tool through the front to create a hole. (*Note: If the tracer is too thick, use a pin.*) Gently press the tip of the tracer into the hole to pierce the pewter.

10. Repeat steps 5–9 to complete the second earring.

11. Press the tip of the medium ball tool into the center of all the small flowers that have four petals. This is to create an indentation to hold the glue for the crystals.

12. Glue all the crystals in position, using the set of wax sticks.

Do this by placing the glue onto the pewter, and the crystal onto the glue — there is less chance of getting glue onto the crystal this way.

13. Replace the findings.

Crafter's notes
• If the findings on your earrings aren't silver, replace them with silver ones that are available at bead stores.
• I used spray contact adhesive for this project. It was used as a contact on the circular pieces of pewter (and the earrings), but when working with the thin strips, I only sprayed it onto the back of the pewter strips.
• I used clear, quick-set epoxy glue to adhere the crystals to the pewter.

Spiral-disk necklace

Spirals are soft, round, never-ending designs. You have probably worked out by now they are one of my favorite shapes — I sneak them in everywhere! So it is no surprise that I wear this necklace as often as I can. I used a round, colored, plastic disk that I found at a bead store but any light, firm, round disk will work, and if it doesn't have a hole in the top, drill one. This design is completed in high relief. So, technically, it's really not difficult.

You will need

firm round disk with hole
soft pencil (6B)
tracing paper
pewter
hard board
masking tape
tracer tool or small ball tool
lubricant
3 pieces of felt
hockey-stick tool (see crafter's notes)
medium-size ball tool
paper pencil
beeswax and glass dropper
turpentine
cotton wool
patina
materials for polishing
glue
black leather thong — thickness depends on size of hole in the disk

1. Place the disk onto a piece of tracing paper and draw around it to create a paper pattern. Add $\frac{1}{16}$" (2 mm) around the edges of the circle — this is to allow the pewter to overlap the edge of the disk. Cut out two pieces of pewter from the paper pattern (front and back). Measure the depth and the circumference of the disk, and cut a paper pattern strip according to this measurement. Place it around the disk to check that it is the correct size, and then cut out the pewter strip.

2. Draw the spiral design from page 136 onto the round tracing-paper pattern. Place the pewter, right-side up, onto the hard board. Complete the design as for high relief. Use the hockey stick to mold the design in the shape of the spiral — do not mold out as one big circle. Move the hockey stick between the lines of the spiral. When neatening up on the hard board, do not neaten up on the spiral lines, only neaten up on the edge of the circle. Fill the back with beeswax and clean off excess wax with turpentine.

3. Using the medium-size ball tool, redefine the spiral line. Repeat this step a number of times until the spiral design is quite deep. Remember: not too hard or too fast.

4. Patinate and polish all three pieces of pewter, leaving the patina on for about 5 minutes to allow the spiral line to become dark.

5. Glue the spiral design into position on the disk, folding the pewter over the edge. Run the tracing tool around this edge to smooth out the pewter — the gathers will flatten.

6. Gently press the tracer tool through the hole at the back of the disk, just hard enough to make a raised bump on the front of the pewter, which will indicate the position of the hole. Using the "bump" as a guide, press the tracer

through from the front of the disk to create the hole.

7. Glue the pewter into position on the back of the disk, as in step 5. Now glue the pewter strip around the disk, ensuring that the join is at the top, as the leather thong will hide it.

8. Thread a leather thong through the hole in the disk. Tie the top of the thong according to the length you require for your necklace, or attach a silver clasp of your choice.

Crafter's notes

• I find my blunt paper pencil easier to control than the hockey stick for this design (see Modelling tools: paper pencil, on page 12).

• I prefer to adorn both sides of the disk with the spiral design. That way, if the disk flips over while you are wearing it, it won't matter.

Daisy medallion

The aventurine stone has a very soft and soothing hue, which provides a lovely background color for the pewter daisy design. I have matched the soft green of the aventurine stone disk with sea green and turquoise-colored Japanese seed beads. The pewter has not been patinated or polished, as I wanted the clean color of the silver against the fresh, pale green of the stone.

You will need

1 aventurine, doughnut-shaped disk (or one of your choice)	beeswax and glass dropper
soft pencil (6B)	turpentine
tracing paper	baby powder
piece of pewter	cotton wool
hard board	craft knife and cutting mat
masking tape	glue
tracer tool or small ball tool	flexible beading wire or nylon
lubricant	silver crimp beads
2 pieces of felt	1 silver clasp of your choice
hockey-stick tool	needle-nose pliers
paper pencil	Japanese seed beads

Pewter flower

1. Place the disk onto the tracing paper. Draw around the outside of the disk to make a paper pattern. Trace the daisy flower from page 136 onto the paper pattern.

2. Complete as for high relief. (*Note: Only the centers of the petals have been raised. The outer section of the design is flat.*)

3. Fill with beeswax and clean off excess with turpentine. Clean the front with baby powder and cotton wool — do not patinate or polish.

4. Cut out the daisy shape using a craft knife and cutting mat. Do not cut out the circle in the middle.

5. Glue the daisy into position on the stone disk and allow the glue to set. Rub your finger over the center of the pewter to find the hole in the stone, then carefully push the tracer through the hole. Push the tip of the paper pencil into the hole

created by the tracer tool; gently ease it in deeper, enlarging the hole until it is the right size. Trim off any pewter at the back of the disk with the craft knife.

Beaded necklace

1. Cut two strands of nylon about 8" (20 cm) longer than required for the length of the necklace. (Remember that the necklace needs to be long enough to loop through the stone disk.) Thread the ends of both nylon strands through a silver crimp bead, then through the clasp, and back again through the crimp. Squeeze the crimp closed with the needle-nose pliers. Thread the turquoise beads onto one strand of nylon, tying one bead onto the very end to prevent the others falling off once you are done. Thread the sea green beads onto the second strand of nylon.

2. Cut the bead off the end of the first strand and trim both strands of nylon to the same length. Thread the ends of both nylon strands through a silver crimp bead, then through the clasp and back again through the crimp. Pull the free ends of the nylon threads until the crimp and clasp are in the correct position, and then squeeze the crimp closed with the pliers.

3. Loop the necklace through the hole in the stone disk (as shown below).

Crafter's note

• It isn't necessary to adorn both sides of this disk, as it will not swing around when worn because of the way it is attached to the necklace.

Pewter-adorned beads

Although we cannot make beads with pewter relief modeling, we can create exclusive designer beads. You can either adorn individual beads and then create your own piece of jewelry, or find ready-strung necklaces to decorate. Flat beads are the easiest to work with. I have used craft punches to create the designs on most of the beads in these projects. Don't worry if you cannot find the exact same beads as the ones I have used: you have the basic idea, so any beautiful, similar-shaped beads of your choice will work.

Of course, it does help to have friends in high places. Once I had adorned the beads, I gave them to Kathleen Barry, the author of Bead Projects and owner of The Bead Studio, who designed and strung the necklaces and bracelet.

Turquoise bead bracelet

I fell madly in love with these reconstructed turquoise beads when I spotted them. It was one of those "just have to have" moments. I wanted to adorn them with pewter, but obviously the pewter decoration had to enhance, rather than detract from, the beads' original beauty. I placed a pewter border around the beads and used the leaf craft-punch design for the decorations. I then added more detail to the leaves with indented low-relief veins. This meant doing the polishing process on the punched-out leaves, as I wanted the black polish to enhance the veins. A little tricky, but not too difficult. An experienced and talented beader designed the bracelet, which really finished off the project and created, what I think is one of the most beautiful bracelets I have seen.

ADORNING THE TURQUOISE BEADS

You will need

3 square, reconstructed
   turquoise beads
pewter
cutting mat

patina
materials for polishing
tracer tool
craft punch (leaf design)
glue

1. The pewter strips are $^5/_{16}$" (8 mm) wide, and the length of the circumference of your bead. It is easier to patinate and polish the pewter before cutting individual strips from it. Once cut, glue them into position around the bead (see crafter's notes). Run the side of the tracer tool around the edges of the pewter border to mold the pewter to the edge of the beads.

2. The pewter will form an indentation over the hole in the bead. Push the tip of the tracer through the pewter to re-create the hole.

3. Punch out six leaves from a piece of pewter. Place each leaf,

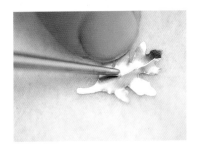

right-side up, onto the cutting mat and, using the tracer tool, "draw" veins onto it. *(Note: You will need one leaf for the front and one for the back of the bead.)*

4. Patinate and polish each leaf, then glue into position on the bead (see crafter's notes).

Crafter's notes

• Ensure that the join of the pewter border is close to one of the holes on the bead, so the join will not be visible once the bracelet is strung.
• You will note that the leaves are positioned on the beads at different angles — this adds a little more interest to the design. You may find it easier to glue the leaves in position after you have strung the bracelet.

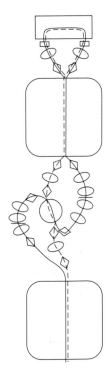

BRACELET

You will need

3 large beads with pewter finishing
16 Swarovski crystals ($^5/_{32}$" or 4 mm)
24 turquoise beads ($^1/_4$" or 6 mm)
4 daisy spacers
2 Bali silver beads ($^5/_{16}$" or 8 mm)
magnetic clasp
4 crimp beads
$15^3/_4$" or 40 cm tiger tail
crimping tool

1. Cut tiger tail in half and attach to clasp as shown in diagram. Attach crimp beads on both sides.
2. Working with two strands, string the beads as follows:
  a. Strand 1: 1 x turquoise, 1 x Swarovski.
  b. Strand 2: 1 x turquoise, 1 x Swarovski.
  c. Both strands through a large bead.
  d. Strand 1: 1 x Swarovski, 2 x turquoise, 1 x spacer, 1 x Swarovski.
  e. Strand 2: 1 x Swarovski, 1 x turquoise, 1 x Swarovski.
  f. Insert strands from opposite sides through bali silver bead (strand 1 from bottom to top, strand 2 from top to bottom).
3. Repeat d, e and c twice.
4. Finish off with 1 x Swarovski, 1 x turquoise on each strand, and attach the other side of the clasp with crimp beads.

Carnelian & pewter bead necklace

All seven beads started off like the three plain brown beads on this necklace. The brown beads are semiprecious carnelian stone. I have done a variety of designs on the four adorned beads (working with their elegant straight lines) to give you some ideas. The bead on the bottom-left, below, has been decorated with a plain piece of pewter: all I have done to this piece of pewter is patinate and polish it, and yet it brings a stylish elegance to the original bead. I have decorated only the large rectangular beads — the others were bought in a bead store.

ADORNING THE BROWN BEADS

You will need

6 flat, rectangular beads of your
   choice
tracing paper
soft pencil (6B)
pewter
hard board
masking tape
patina
materials for polishing
1 piece of felt
tracer or small ball tool
ruler
paper pencil
craft punches (various designs)
glue

1. Cut a paper pattern to fit the beads. (*Note: The pewter will need to be cut to fit the bead from the top to the bottom. Also, allow enough pewter to wrap all the way around the bead.*) Cut four pieces of pewter this size. Patinate and polish all four pieces of pewter.

2. For bead one, place the pewter, wrong-side up, onto a piece of felt. Secure the pewter with masking tape. Using the tracer tool and a ruler, "draw" a line about $\frac{1}{8}$" (3 mm) from the edge of the pewter. (*Note: Make sure you are working on the pewter edge that will run down the length of the bead.*) Turn the pewter over, right-side up, and place onto the hard board. Run the paper pencil down each side of the raised line to flatten the pewter on each side of the line. If you want the line raised a little more, repeat this step. Create the raised low-relief line on the opposite side of the piece of pewter as well, so the design will be on the front and the back of the bead (see crafter's notes). Glue in position on the bead.

3. For the second bead, you will need the heart craft punch. Place the edge of the pewter into the

punch and hold the punch up-side down so that you can see the position of the pewter in the punch. Ensure that the pewter

is covering only *half* the blade, as we only want to cut out half the heart. Punch out the design. (*Note: Keep this "heart half" in a safe place.*) Repeat this step for the other side of the pewter, to create a front and back for your bead.

4. Now glue the pewter into position on the bead. Place the first "heart half" in position on the bead so that it completes the heart design — you will need to turn it

over so the wrong side of the pewter is showing – and glue down. Repeat this for the other side of the bead.

5. Repeat step 3 for the punched-out leaf pattern, using the leaf craft punch instead.

6. The fourth bead has no design on it. Simply glue the pewter into position on the bead.

7. String the beads, combining them with other beads to form a pleasing combination.

Crafter's notes
• Decorate the front and the back of the beads, as they may flip over while you are wearing the necklace.
• It is easier to patinate and polish the pewter before punching out the designs, because you are working with a large piece of pewter.
• This is a good opportunity to use up your pewter remnants.

Crystal-adorned carnelian bead

This is a lovely, simple design. I have used the same craft punch here as I use for the long-stemmed candle sticks on page 110.

ADORNING THE BEAD

You will need

1 flat, rectangular bead of your
   choice
pewter
craft knife and cutting mat
ruler
patina
materials for polishing
craft punch
5 flatback crystals (size ss5)
glue
set of wax sticks (see instructions
   on page 59)

1. Cut out a piece of pewter to fit the length of the bead, but cut it about ⅜" (1 cm) wider than necessary. (*Note: It is easier to handle a larger piece of pewter when using the punch.*) Patinate and polish the piece of pewter. Punch out the design, holding the craft punch upside down to enable you to see the position of the pewter in the punch.

2. Using a craft knife, cutting mat and ruler, trim the piece of pewter to the required width, and glue into position on the bead.

3. Glue the flatbacked crystals into position on the pewter using the wax sticks.

Crafter's note
• It is best to adorn both sides of the bead with the design, as the bead will swivel around when the necklace is worn.

Wooden cross

This little wooden cross has an endearing, irregular shape. The right-hand side of the cross bar is wider than the left-hand side. As someone who does not enjoy straight lines and loves a bit of imperfection, I found the little cross charming. I have adorned it in a fairly rough and rugged way to retain the original rustic character.

You will need

wooden cross
flatback black stone (or color of
   your choice)
tracing paper
soft pencil (6B)
pewter
1 piece of felt
hard board
masking tape
medium-size ball tool
lubricant
paper pencil
tracer tool or small ball tool
patina
cotton wool
materials for polishing
silver cord or thong
glue

1. Trace the design from page 136 onto tracing paper. Place the stone in position on the paper, and draw around it with a pencil to get the exact shape and size of your stone. Now cut the cross out of pewter.
2. Place the pewter cross, wrong-side up, onto a piece of felt. Complete the circle as for raised low-relief, using the medium-size ball tool.
3. Place pewter, right-side up, onto a single layer of felt. Use the tracer tool to indent the dots.
4. Patinate and polish. (*Note: I left the patina on for 10 minutes so that the pewter would be quite dark.*)

5. Glue the pewter cross into position on the wooden cross. Glue the stone down in place too.
6. Thread the cord through the top of the cross and knot it according to your length requirements.

Crafter's notes
• If you have a light-colored cross, paint it with antique oak wood stain to darken the wood.
• Resize the design on a photo-copier to fit your cross.
• I used clear, quick-set epoxy glue to adhere the stone to the pewter.

Blackboard tins

Blackboard tins provide great storage in kitchens, children's bedrooms and workshops. The blackboard labels are good places to write warning notes to the cookie thief! With the aid of a damp cloth and piece of chalk, you can regularly rename the tin according to the contents. The idea will also work for the lids of tins that do not have as much height.

You will need

tin(s)
permanent marker
ruler
masking tape
paintbrush
gray metal primer
blackboard paint
tracing paper
soft pencil (6B)
pewter
craft knife and cutting mat
2 pieces of felt
hard board
tracer tool
lubricant
hockey-stick tool
paper pencil
beeswax
glass dropper
turpentine
lubricant
cotton wool
patina
materials for polishing
glue

1. Make sure the tin is clean and free of dust and grease. Using the permanent marker and a ruler, draw the rectangle onto the tin that will be painted black. *(Note: It should be larger than the inside of the pewter frame, but smaller than the outside of it.)*

2. Place masking tape around the outer edges of the rectangle. Press the masking tape down well, so that no paint gets underneath it.

3. Paint inside the masked area with the metal primer. When dry, paint with blackboard paint and leave that to dry.

4. Trace the pewter design from page 137 onto the tracing paper; then trace onto the pewter. Cut away the inside of the frame using the craft knife (this can be used for another project).

5. Complete the design of the large tin in indented low-relief.

6. The heart design of the small tin is to be completed in high relief. Fill with wax and clean off any excess with turpentine. Retrace the designs on the heart.

7. Patinate and polish both designs and glue into place on the tins.

Crafter's note
• If your metal primer is in an aerosol can, ensure that the areas of the tin that are not being painted are securely covered with paper.

Kissing-cow blackboard

This adorable kissing-cow blackboard will suit any kitchen, from farmhouse to contemporary. Blackboards are very popular in French decor, and, personally, I think they are a great idea.

Technically this design is challenging, but if you have mastered the high-relief techniques you will manage fine — just work slowly and carefully.

You will need

blackboard
tracing paper
soft pencil (6B)
pewter
hard board
masking tape
tracer tool
lubricant
4 pieces of felt

teaspoon
hockey-stick tool
medium-size ball tool
paper pencil
beeswax and glass dropper
turpentine
cotton wool
patina
materials for polishing

glue
black glass paint
soft, pointed watercolor brush
acetone (check instructions on glass
   paint bottle for solvent required
   — most use acetone)
cotton swabs
hammer
6 silver nails

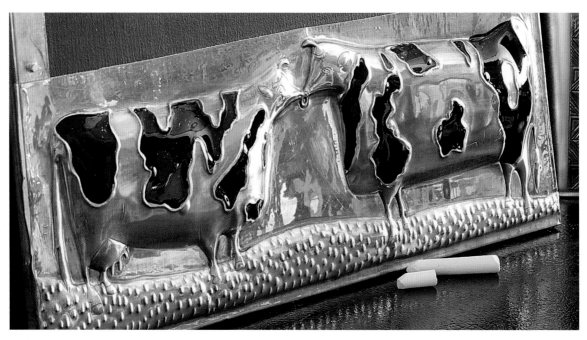

1. Measure and cut three paper patterns for the pewter frame. Remember to allow extra for the edge of the blackboard and a $3/8$" (1 cm) overlap at the back of the board. The top corners of the frame meet at 45-degree angles. Cut a pattern piece for the section with the cow design, remembering to include the overlap. (*Note: I have used four separate pieces of pewter, three for the frame and one for the bottom cow design.*) Using these paper patterns, cut out the pewter pieces.

2. Trace the design from page 137 onto the paper pattern for the cow piece. Place the pewter, right-side up, onto the hard board. Complete the design as for high relief. (*Note: Do not trace the grass; it is far easier to do this freehand.*)

3. Start the sculpturing process by molding the grassed hill out a little, and then move on to the cows and do the same. Build all three areas together. When neatening up the top of the hill with the paper pencil, you will need to work between the cows' legs — do not run the paper pencil over the legs. Define the bottom section of the cows' legs on top of the grassed hill only once the wax is in.

4. Once the design is the right height and shape, place it wrong-side up onto one layer of felt. Using the medium-size ball tool, draw in the grass on the hill. Still using the medium-size ball tool, draw all around the black markings on the cows' bodies, including where the

markings continue to the edge of the body. We are raising the edges of the black markings to create "dam walls" to hold the black glass paint.

5. Fill the back of the design with beeswax — it will need a lot. Clean off excess wax with turpentine (see crafter's notes).

6. Use the tracer tool to redefine the facial features of the cows, the bits of the legs that are on the hill, the tail hairs and the areas where the legs meet the body. Define the raised markings on the cows' bodies. Do not define around the blades of grass.

7. Patinate and polish all four sections of pewter.

8. Glue the pewter into position on the frame and trim it at the bottom corners, folding the excess pewter over the frame.

9. Dip the brush into the black glass paint and allow the paint to

flow between the raised lines. The brush will need to be quite loaded with paint. Clean the brush regularly in the acetone, as the paint dries quickly and clogs the brush. Clean off any paint spills outside the lines with a cotton swab dipped in acetone.

10. Once the paint is completely dry, use the hammer to knock in the silver nails on the pewter frame.

Crafter's notes

• If you do not have the correct size blackboard, ask your local hardware store to cut a piece of wood to size, and paint it with blackboard paint.

• If you happen to push through the pewter when molding, don't worry too much. The wax will close up the hole. Fill up with wax as usual, but once the wax has solidified you will need to clean the front of the design, because some of it will have seeped through the hole. Once clean, use your paper pencil to push the torn pewter into place.

• You will need to reheat the wax a few times during the filling process, as it will cool down during the time it takes to fill the design. If the wax starts clogging in the dropper, it means it is too cold, so reheat. Take care, as the wax can ignite if overheated.

• One way of keeping the wax hot a little longer is to heat it to the required temperature and then place it on top of a double boiler (or stand the can of wax in a bowl of boiling water). It is also best to work with about three to four glass droppers.

Art deco glass bowl

This is one of my favorite designs and it is not difficult technically. I have built up "dam walls" to hold the glass paints using raised low-relief. The design will also work well on a picture frame or the lid of a wooden box or tin, and is an interesting alternative to the design on the white serving plate on page 94 and the salad servers on page 96.

You will need

glass bowl (or item of choice)

tracing paper

soft pencil (6B)

pewter

1 piece of felt

hard board

masking tape

medium ball tool

lubricant

paper pencil

patina

cotton wool

materials for polishing

soft, pointed watercolor paintbrush

glass paints: amber, green, blue, deep red and purple (or colors of your choice)

acetone (check this is the solvent for your brand of glass paint)

glue

1. Draw your design onto tracing paper. (*Note: I have not put the design in the book, as you will need to draw this one freehand so that it fits your item. Fill up the pewter area with squares and rectangles, drawn without a ruler.*)

2. Complete the design as for raised low-relief. Make sure the low-relief design lines are quite high, because they need to hold the paint. You may need to take them out two or three times with the ball tool, neatening up with the paper pencil on either side of the design line each time.

3. Patinate and polish. (*Note: I left the patina on for 10 minutes because I wanted the metal dark, but the choice is yours.*)

4. Dip the brush into the color of paint required, and paint the squares by allowing the paint to flow between the raised lines. Make sure there is a lot of paint on the brush. As you move the brush around the inside of the shapes, the paint will flow into these areas.

5. Allow the paints to dry completely: they are hard when dry.

6. Glue the pewter design onto the bowl, cleaning away any excess glue.

Crafter's notes

• To cut a perfect circle, it is best to cut around a template. Place the pewter onto a cutting mat; then place the glass bowl upside down onto the pewter and cut around the bowl with a sharp craft knife. Search the kitchen for a plate or dish of the right size to use as a template for the smaller inner circle.

• I have placed pewter on the flat edge of the bowl only. As the glass dips toward the inner area of the bowl, the bowl becomes smaller — placing pewter on this area will result in the pewter gathering.

• Clean off the paintbrush regularly, as the paint dries quickly and clogs the brush.

• Clean the brush in acetone before using a different color.

Classic white serving dish

Silver and white represent timeless elegance, and I have kept to the clean, straight lines of the serving platter. Technically this is a very simple design, and therefore a good start after completing the beginner's exercises. The leaves and flowers are done in high relief, and the stems in indented low-relief.

You will need

white serving platter with a flat, broad edge
tracing paper
soft pencil (6B)
pewter
hard board
masking tape
tracer tool
lubricant
2 pieces of felt
hockey-stick tool
paper pencil
beeswax and glass dropper
turpentine
cotton wool
patina
materials for polishing
glue

1. For this project I have included a large overlap of pewter to turn underneath the dish. It is equal to the amount of pewter on top of the dish, so remember to add the overlap to your paper pattern. Cut a tracing-paper pattern for all four sides of the dish, cutting the edges at a 45-degree angle. Place the paper patterns onto the dish to ensure that they are the correct size. Now cut the pewter out using the patterns.

2. Trace the design from page 138 onto your paper pattern pieces, and then trace the designs onto the pewter. Place the pewter, right-side up, onto the hard board. Complete the flowers and leaves as for high relief, and the stems as for indented low-relief.

3. Patinate and polish.

4. Glue the pewter onto the serving dish and press down well (see crafter's notes).

Crafter's notes

• Cut four separate strips of pewter, to be joined at 45-degree angles at the corners of the serving dish. This is more economical than cutting a large rectangle of pewter.

• I used spray contact adhesive on this project. If you use it, remember to cover the area that is not to be glued with paper. Allow the contact adhesive the full drying time before placing the pewter onto the dish. The glue will feel as if it will not stick, but press down firmly and allow about 2 hours for the glue to set, before cleaning away excess glue with turpentine.

Salad servers

These salad servers were made from a light-colored wood. How-ever, I prefer a dark, contrasting color with the white serving dish, so I painted the wooden servers with antique oak wood stain. This is good way to revive and re-create any tired old salad servers lying at the bottom of the drawer.

You will need

set of wooden serving spoons
fine sandpaper
antique oak stain
satin-finish water-based varnish
paintbrush
tracing paper
soft pencil (6B)
pewter
hard board
masking tape
tracer tool
lubricant
2 pieces of felt
hockey-stick tool
paper pencil
beeswax and glass dropper
turpentine
cotton wool
patina
materials for polishing
glue

1. Lightly sand the salad servers, wipe clean and paint with two coats of stain. Allow to dry, then apply two coats of varnish.
2. Place the handle of a salad server onto a piece of tracing paper, and draw around it to create a pattern. Add $\frac{1}{16}''$ (2 mm) to the size of the overall pattern (see crafter's notes). Trace a section of the flower-and-leaf design from page 138 onto the pattern. A little artistic license may be needed to get the pattern to fit the handles of your salad servers.
3. Cut the handle shape out of pewter using the paper pattern. You will need two pieces of pewter per handle: a back and a front.
4. Place the pewter, right-side up, onto the hard board. Complete the flower-and-leaf designs as for high relief. Complete the stem as for indented low-relief.
5. Patinate and polish.
6. To cover the edge of the handle, measure the depth of it and cut one long strip to this width. Ensure that the strip is long enough to reach all around the pewtered area of the handle. (*Note: You will need two strips, one for each server.*) Patinate and polish both strips.
7. Glue the front and back pieces onto the handles first. Fold the pewter over the edge and press down well. Now glue the long strip of pewter around the handle. Use the craft knife to trim all three pieces of pewter to the same length where they meet at the bottom of the handle.

Crafter's notes

• You can mold the design on the front and back of the handles, or just on the front.
• The piece of pewter you cut for the handle needs to be slightly larger than the actual handle, to allow the pewter to overlap the sides slightly. This is to ensure there are no gaps between the front and back pieces of pewter and the strip that runs around the edge of the handle.
• If the salad servers have a hole in the top of the handle, cover the handles as described in step 7, then rub your finger over the top of the handle to find the hole. Carefully push the tracer tool through the hole to pierce the pewter. Push the tip of the paper pencil into the hole created by the tracer and gently ease it in deeper, enlarging the hole in the pewter until it is the size of the original. Repeat for the hole at the back of the handle.

Cheese board

This is a classic, simple design for a cheese board. All we need to add is a bottle of wine and some sunshine. I was lucky enough to find a bamboo board with a lovely texture, but beautiful wooden boards are not hard to find. This is a great way to reinvent one of your own well-used wooden boards. The design is completed in high relief.

You will need

wooden board
tracing paper
soft pencil (6B)
pewter
craft knife and cutting mat
hard board
masking tape
tracer tool or small ball tool
lubricant
2 pieces of felt
teaspoon
hockey-stick tool
paper pencil
beeswax and glass dropper
turpentine
cotton wool
patina
materials for polishing
glue

1. Place the edge of the board onto the tracing paper and draw around it with a pencil. This will give you a paper pattern. Trace the design from page 138 onto the pattern piece: center the design and keep it close to the drawn pencil line, as this represents the edge of the board.

2. Cut the pewter from the paper pattern, but remember to allow for the side of the wooden board and a $^3/_8$" (1 cm) overlap at the back of the board (see crafter's notes).

3. Place pewter, right-side up, onto the hard board. Trace the design using the tracer or small ball tool. Complete the design as for high relief. Use the teaspoon to mold out the leaf, the hockey stick to mold the grapes, and the paper pencil to mold the stems.

4. Fill the back with beeswax, and clean off any excess wax with turpentine.

5. Place pewter, right-side up, onto the hard board. Using the tracer tool, retrace the veins of the leaves.

6. Patinate and polish.

7. Repeat these steps to complete the second side. Make sure the grape design is facing the correct way on your pattern — place the pattern onto the board to check.

8. Using a craft knife and cutting mat, cut out part of the leaf and part of the grapes (see photo). All the grapes that I have deep-etched are still attached to the main design.

9. Glue the design onto the board and trim the corners to fit (see photographs on page 91). Fold the edge over, and underneath, the board. Press down well.

Crafter's notes

• Try the paper pattern on the wooden board to make sure it fits, before cutting out the pewter. Paper patterns are invaluable. By making a paper pattern first, you will eliminate errors and thereby save a lot of time and pewter.

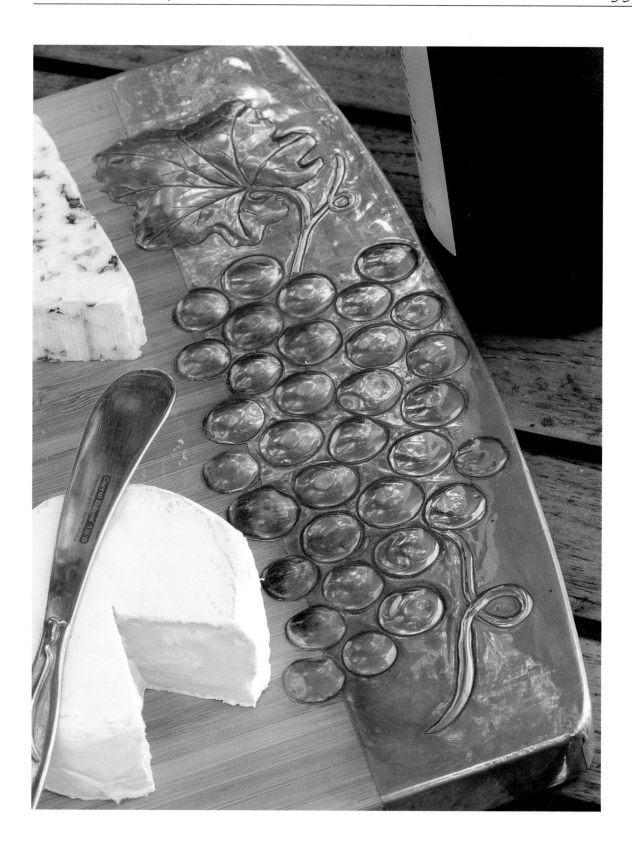

Pewter sushi plate

A round design on a square plate, why not? This design changes the look of the plate completely. The black plate in this project gives a very "sushi" feel to the design. If you can't find a black plate, don't worry — white or any other color will work.

You will need

square black plate (about 11" x 11"
    or 28 cm x 28 cm)
tracing paper
soft pencil (6B)
pewter: $3/8$" or 1 cm larger than plate
craft knife and cutting mat
hard board
masking tape
tracer tool
lubricant
2 pieces of felt
hockey-stick tool
paper pencil
beeswax and glass dropper
turpentine
cotton wool
patina
materials for polishing
gold permanent marker

1. Place the black plate onto the tracing paper, and, using a pencil, draw around it. Draw a circle in the center of the square (approximately 9" or 23 cm diameter). Trace the fish design from page 139 onto all four corners, and the fishtail design between each fish.
2. Cut the inner circle out of the pewter square.
3. Place the pewter, right-side up, onto the hard board. Complete the designs as for high relief.
4. Fill the back of the design with beeswax. Leave to harden, and clean off excess wax with turpentine.
5. Using the tracer tool, retrace the fish scales and fin details, and redefine the design lines on either side of the gills, as well as the raised line between the tail and body. Gently indent the pupil with the tip of the tracer.

6. Patinate and polish.
7. Glue pewter into position on the plate. Turn the plate over, trim the pewter corners (see photographs on page 91), and neatly fold over the excess pewter.
8. Using the gold permanent marker, draw on the gills, the eye and the line above the tail. If the gold marker scrapes away when dry, reapply, and when dry, apply a little water-based varnish over it.

Crafter's note
• To cut a perfect circle, it is best to cut around a template. Find the correct size plate or dish, place the pewter onto a cutting mat, place the plate on top of the pewter and cut around it using a craft knife.

Knife & fork holder

This is an effective, yet technically simple, project, completed in high relief. The wording can be done on a computer and then printed out and traced onto tracing paper. It is best to choose a font that is not too intricate: I have used Arial Black. The wording is placed on opposite sides of the holder, and the picture design is used on the two remaining sides.

You will need

MDF knife and fork holder
pewter
black craft paint
paintbrush
fine sandpaper
tracing paper
soft pencil (6B)
hard board
masking tape
tracer tool
lubricant
2 pieces of felt
hockey-stick tool
paper pencil
beeswax and glass dropper
turpentine
cotton wool
patina
materials for polishing
glue

1. Cut out four pieces of pewter to correspond with the size and shape of the four sides of the knife and fork holder.
2. Paint the holder with the black craft paint and allow to dry completely. Sand all over with fine sandpaper. Apply another coat of black paint and leave to dry.
3. For the knife and fork, place the pewter, right-side up, onto the hard board. Trace the design of the knife and fork from page 144 onto the pewter. Complete as for high relief.
4. Fill the back with beeswax and clean off excess with turpentine. Retrace the spiral design at the bottom of the handles using the tracer tool.
5. Patinate and polish.
6. I have completed the words "Knives & Forks" in high relief.

7. Duplicate each design on another piece of pewter so that you have four sides.
8. Glue all four designs onto the sides of the knife and fork holder.

Crafter's notes
• If the handle of the knife and fork holder is removable, you can cover it in pewter. Have a look at the handle of the woven teaspoon caddy on page 107.

Woven teaspoon caddy

As far as I know, this technique is revolutionary in pewter craft. Weaving with pewter is not part of the traditional craft, which is what makes it so exciting. A student of mine, Birga Thomas, who is a very experienced weaver, asked if it was possible to weave with strips of pewter. Of course I had never considered this. So straight after the lesson I sat down to work it out. I think the effect is wonderful. The written step-by-step instructions might sound a little complicated, but it is not that difficult; it's quite logical. If you have ever done paper weaving, you will find that the technique is very much the same.

You will need

MDF teaspoon caddy
oil-based, dark-colored wood
   varnish
paintbrush
fine sandpaper
tracing paper
soft pencil (6B)
pewter
craft knife and cutting mat
1 piece of felt
steel ruler
tracer tool

hard board
masking tape
paper pencil
beeswax and glass dropper
turpentine
cotton wool
patina
materials for polishing
felt-tip marker
glue
stove polish

Crafter's note
• The picture frame above has been completed using the same weaving technique as for the woven teaspoon caddy.

1. Paint the teaspoon caddy with the wood varnish and allow to dry completely. Sand with fine sandpaper and apply another two coats of varnish, sanding between coats. Leave to dry.

2. Cut out four pieces of pewter to correspond with the size and shape of the sides of the caddy.

3. We are going to work on one side at a time, starting with one of the two largest sides. Place the pewter, right-side up, onto a single layer of felt. The border lines running down the side of the pewtered area are done in indented low-relief; do this using the tracer tool and a ruler. The border is $3/16$" (5 mm) away from the edge of the caddy. Remove the layer of felt, and, using the tracer, draw four circles that are evenly spaced down the inside of the border.

4. Turn the pewter over, wrong-side up, onto a single layer of felt, and complete the circles as for high relief. Fill with wax. Patinate and polish the entire piece of pewter.

5. Place the pewter, right-side up, onto a cutting mat. Place masking tape down the indented border line on each end of the pewter.

Using a felt-tip marker, mark off $3/16$" (5 mm) intervals on the masking tape. Mark the tape on both ends of the pewter, as this ensures the lines will be cut straight.

6. Use the steel ruler and craft knife to cut across the piece of pewter, using the felt-tip markings opposite each other to guide you. Continue all the way down your piece of pewter. (*Note: Do not cut over the masking tape — the pewter still remains in one piece.*)

7. Measure the piece of pewter you are working on and divide the width measurement by two. Add $3/4$" (2 cm) to the height measurement and cut a piece of pewter to this measurement. (My piece of pewter measured $5^1/2$" in width by $3^1/8$" in height, or 140 mm x 80 mm, so I cut a piece of pewter $2^3/4$" x $3^7/8$". or 70 mm x 100 mm.) Patinate and polish this piece of pewter.

8. Cut this piece of pewter into $3/16$" (5 mm) strips. (My strips measured $3/16$" x $3^7/8$", or 5 mm x 100 mm.)

9. Weave a single strip of pewter through the large piece of pewter; do this by continuously weaving it *over and under* the cross strips. Now butt the woven single strip up against the solid edge of the large piece of pewter.

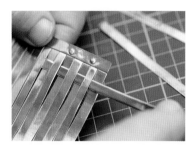

10. Weave a second, single strip of pewter through the large piece of pewter. This time, go *under and over* the cross strips. Push the second piece of pewter up to the first piece. Continue until the entire piece is woven.

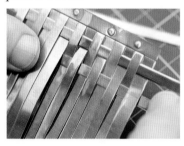

11. Every second single strip of pewter will end on top of the cross strip. Trim these pieces of pewter and fold them over to the back of the large piece of pewter. (It's not necessary to stick them down.)

12. The alternate single strips will end underneath the cross strips. Cut these pieces flush with the top of the large piece of pewter.

Lift them away from the pewter, place a tiny dot of glue on the tip of each strip and stick down.

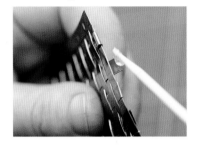

13. Polish the completed woven piece with stove polish. This will give added depth to the woven pattern, as black polish will sit between the woven pieces of pewter.

14. Repeat the process from step 3 to step 13 on the other three pieces of pewter.

15. Adhere the four pieces of woven pewter to the sides of the teaspoon caddy.

16. Cut four strips of pewter to size, to place on the top edges of the teaspoon caddy. (*Note: It is easier to polish the piece of pewter before cutting it into the four strips.*)

17. The handle of my teaspoon caddy was removable, so it was easy to cut its shape from pewter. I used the handle as a template, cut pewter for both sides, patinated and polished the pewter, and then glued it in place. I cut strips for the side (and the inside) oval of the handle, then patinated and polished them before gluing them in place. I then glued the handle securely back in place in the caddy. However, the handle does not have to be covered in pewter; it may be left as is, just sanded and varnished.

Crafter's notes

• You may find there is not enough space to weave the last strip of pewter. If this is the case, trim a little pewter off the side of the strip. So instead of it measuring ³/₁₆" (5 mm) in width, it will measure about ⁵/₃₂" (4 mm). Trust me, no one will notice the odd missing fraction of pewter.

• The two narrow sides of my caddy are wider at the top than at the bottom. This makes it a little tricky. I wove the pewter in the same manner as the symmetrical sides, but cut the single strips slightly narrower at the bottom. The top of the strips measure ³/₁₆" (5 mm), but they measure about ⅛" (3.5 mm) at the bottom. I must be honest; working out the mathematical ratio was not my idea of fun, so it was a guess. There was not enough space in the cross strips for the last single strip to be woven all the way to the bottom, so I wove it as far as I could and then cut it off at the back. Visually it works perfectly — this is known as artistic license ...

Naked chefs

Salt and pepper grinders

Either I have an awesome imagination, or I am in desperate need of good food cooked by somebody other than me. But when I spotted these salt and pepper grinders, the silver tops looked just like chefs' hats waiting for their chefs to be born. The pewter look-alike tops help to complete the picture, but black, white or wooden tops will look just as good.

This is technically a very simple design, completed in indented low-relief with just the male chef's nipples done in raised low-relief. Low relief works best on this project because it doesn't change the shape of the grinders; instead, it enhances their long, sleek look.

Trace the designs from page 140 onto tracing paper, holding the paper in place on each grinder to make sure that it fits. Adjust accordingly — it is easy to extend or shorten the legs. Complete the designs using the low-relief techniques, then patinate and polish. Cut the shapes out using a pair of nail scissors, with the curve of the scissors facing away from the design line.

It gets a little tricky cutting around the neck areas, so you might find it easier to use a craft knife and cutting mat for these parts. Leave a little extra pewter (approximately $1/8$" or 3 mm) at the top and bottom of the designs when cutting out.

Glue the chefs in place, then fold the extra bit of pewter over the top and bottom edges of the grinders. This helps to secure the pewter to the grinders and prevents the corners lifting up, especially at the top, as this is a high-use area.

Candlestick

Here is a quick and easy technique, using a craft punch. This was originally a plain glass candlestick and I have only placed pewter around the top. Don't be put off if you cannot find exactly the same candlestick or craft punch. This idea will work on many items, and all craft-punch designs will work with pewter. A clear glass candlestick, designed to hold a tea-light candle, will work well, as the candlelight will shine through the cutout area of the pewter design.

You will need

candlestick
tracing paper
soft pencil (6B)
pewter
patina
cotton wool
materials for polishing
craft punch (design of your choice)
glue (I used spray contact)

1. Measure the top of the candlestick, work out what size the pewter piece needs to be and then cut it out. (*Note: It is safer to cut the pattern out of paper first and wrap the paper around the top of the candlestick to make sure it fits correctly. Once your paper pattern is the correct size, cut the pewter from the pattern.*)

2. Patinate and polish.

3. Using the craft punch, press out the design — you have to press quite hard. Make sure you match up the pattern, and that it is straight, for the second punch-out. Glue the pewter to the candlestick.

Crafter's notes

• For this project I did not allow the pewter to overlap where the two ends meet. You can trim any excess pewter off with a sharp craft knife.

• Because the craft punch has a set design, the pattern will probably not meet correctly at the join. There is no way to overcome this. I don't think it matters with this pattern; most people will never notice that it's not perfect.

• It is easier to patinate and polish before using the craft punch, as the delicate areas of the design tend to get torn and the cotton wool gets caught when polishing.

Bathroom accesories

Add a little shine to your bathroom with some stylish pewter accessories. These are also lovely gift ideas.

I left pieces of pewter in a glass of water for two months — they didn't rust or even discolor, so your pewter projects are quite safe in a steamy bathroom. Look for a soap dispenser that is the same diameter at the top as it is at the bottom, as it will make the task of covering it with pewter so much easier. This Indian design reminded me of a droplet of water, so I thought it would be an appropriate design for something associated with water. The design is done in high relief.

SOAP DISPENSERS

You will need

soap dispenser
tracing paper
soft pencil (6B)
pewter
hard board
masking tape
tracer tool
lubricant
2 pieces of felt
hockey-stick tool
paper pencil
beeswax and glass dropper
turpentine
cotton wool
patina
materials for polishing
glue

1. Cut a piece of tracing paper to fit around the dispenser, in order to make a pattern. Once you are happy that it is the correct size, cut the pewter using the pattern.
2. Trace the design from page 139 onto the tracing paper. Place the pewter, right-side up, onto the hard board
3. Complete the design as for high relief, and fill with wax.
4. Patinate and polish.
5. Glue in place onto the dispenser (see crafter's notes).

Crafter's notes

• I have repeated the Indian "water droplet" on both sides of the dispenser, with the word "Soap" centered between them. The join of the pewter runs down the back of the dispenser.
• The word "Soap" has been done in Arial Black Oblique. I sized it on the computer, printed it, and then traced the word onto tracing paper.
• Do not use water-based glue for this project — the steam in the bathroom will dissolve the glue.

TOOTHBRUSH HOLDER

If you can't find a good toothbrush holder, use a pen and pencil holder. I generally find them better designed to hold toothbrushes and toothpaste tubes anyway. The main area of this design (see page 139) is done in high relief, and the background has been done in indented low-relief. The contrast of the two techniques enhances the design. Use a tracer tool for the background, and do it freehand — it's easier than tracing it. This is a cross-hatching design: I have done three lines up and three lines across. Make sure that you get right up to the high-relief design with the cross-hatching.

Girls' faces mirror

Go big or go home! You've done lots of smaller projects; now it's time to boost your confidence and do something large and substantial that you can hang up proudly and use every day.

The girls' faces almost have a Picasso look to them. I have used only essential lines to draw the faces. I have not sculptured much defining shape into the faces; there is no definition of cheekbones, and very little defining shape around the eyes. The hair is almost helmetlike I love the look of the faces because they are slightly offbeat, being more artistic than realistic.

Technically, this is not as difficult as it looks, as you do not have to sculpture a realistic face. It is all done in high relief, with indented low-relief *on* the high relief. So go ahead — give it a go.

You will need

framed mirror
tracing paper
soft pencil (6B)
pewter
hard board
masking tape
tracer tool or small ball tool
lubricant
5 pieces of felt
teaspoon

hockey-stick tool
medium-size ball tool
paper pencil
beeswax and glass dropper
turpentine
cotton wool
patina
materials for polishing
glue

1. Work out how much pewter is needed to cover each section of the frame, and cut paper patterns from tracing paper accordingly. *(Note: You will need four separate paper patterns, as the frame is made up in four sections — see crafter's notes.)* Remember to allow enough pewter both to fold over the depth of the frame, and to tuck underneath it. There will

also need to be enough pewter to fold over the depth of the frame on the inside (toward the mirror). Place your patterns on the frame to make sure the sizes are correct, before cutting the pewter.

2. Cut out the four pieces of pewter using your paper patterns, and set aside. Trace the designs from page 141 onto the tracing-paper patterns. Now begin working on the girl on the right.

3. Place the pewter, right-side up, onto the hard board. Trace the design onto the pewter using the tracer tool. Complete the design as for high relief. You will use the teaspoon for most of the design. Remember to mold the pewter out very slowly — these are large designs so the pewter will stretch very quickly. The neck area is much narrower than the face area, so it cannot stretch out as far. This is an area to watch for buckling: if the face is pushed out too much compared to the neck, the area where the face and neck join will buckle. Do not shape the eye. Use the hockey stick to mold the lips.

4. Once the face, neck and chest are pushed out enough, you can start sculpturing the hair, necklace and breast. These are your second levels. (Simply mold them. Do not define these levels until the wax is in.) Use the hockey stick to mold the spiral shape of the breast. Mold it out in the shape of the spiral, not as a raised circle.

5. Fill with wax. It takes a lot of wax, so be patient, it will take a little time to fill (see crafter's notes). Clean off any excess wax with turpentine.

6. Using the tracer tool, retrace the eyes, eyebrows, hairline, lips and necklace. Using the medium-size ball tool, retrace the spiral on the breast.

7. Patinate and polish.

8. Repeat steps 3–7 for the girl on the left.

9. Place the pewter for the bottom of the frame, right-side up, onto the hard board. Trace the heart-and-leaf design onto the pewter. Complete as for high relief. Use the teaspoon for most of the design. However, you will need to mold out the corners with the paper pencil.

10. Fill with wax and clean off excess with turpentine.

11. Place pewter, right-side up, onto hard board. Use the medium-size ball tool to retrace the spirals on the heart, and use the tracer to retrace the veins on the leaves.

12. Patinate and polish.

13. Repeat steps 9–12 for the top section of the frame, using the rosebud-and-leaf design.

14. Glue the top and bottom strips onto the frame first, folding the pewter over the edge and to the back of the frame. Trim the pewter to fold over the corners of the frame (see pictures on page 91).

15. Now glue the side strips onto the frame, folding the pewter over the edge and to the back of the frame. Trim the pewter to fold over the corners of the frame, as you did for the first two strips.

Crafter's notes

• I found a framed mirror at a home store with the perfect flat, broad frame. If you cannot find one like this, get a mirror cut to size and have it framed. Remember to keep the frame simple — it must be flat, not bevelled.

• I have not cut the pewter frame pieces to meet at 45-degree angles at the corners. Instead, I cut the top and bottom pewter pieces long enough to go right across the frame, from edge to edge. The vertical strips (with the face designs) are shorter, having been cut to fit between the horizontal ones.

• You will need to reheat the wax a few times during the filling process, as it will cool down during the time it takes to fill the design. If the wax starts clogging in the dropper, it is too cold, so you need to reheat. Take care, as the wax can ignite if overheated. (See Kissing-cow blackboard on page 91 for reheating tips.)

Vintage bedside table

With rose design

> Won't you come into my garden?
> I would like my Roses to see you.
> Anon

The bedside table has a lovely "olde worlde" feel to it. The soft femininity of the rose design works well with the vintage feel of the table.

Try to find a bedside table with a door that has an inset panel like the one I have used, as this gives the pewter a natural frame, and you don't end up with a piece of pewter that just looks "stuck on." If you don't have an inset panel, you can avoid the "stuck on" look by gluing a wooden beading frame around the pewter.

The rose design is completed mostly in high relief. Not all the areas are the same height, however, so it is time to use a few sculpturing techniques. Try it; it is not as difficult as it looks.

You will need

wooden bedside table
tracing paper
soft pencil (6B)
pewter
hard board
masking tape
tracer tool or small ball tool
lubricant
3 pieces of felt

hockey-stick tool
paper pencil
beeswax and glass dropper
turpentine
cotton wool
patina
polishing materials
black stove polish
contact adhesive

1. Make a paper pattern from tracing paper to fit the panel on the bedside-table door. Cut the pewter using the paper pattern. Trace the design from page 142 onto the tracing-paper pattern. Place the pewter, right-side up, onto the hard board. Trace the entire design onto the pewter (see crafter's notes).

2. Complete as for high relief. The centers of the roses are lower than the surrounding petals. I have kept the design lines around all the petals at surface level. So when neatening up on the hard board, draw around all the petals with the paper pencil. I have molded the leaves as two halves, making the center vein the lowest area of the leaf. The calyx (outer covering) of the rosebuds must be higher than the petals of the rosebuds. The extended tips of the rosebuds and the thorns on the stems are completed in indented low-relief. I used a medium-size ball tool, instead of the tracer tool, for the final neatening up on the roses — this creates a slightly wider design line around the petals. The tracer tool was used for the final neatening up around all the other areas.

3. Fill with beeswax and clean off excess with turpentine. Place the pewter, right-side up, onto the hard board, redefine the veins on the leaves, and redefine the calyxes on the rosebuds with the tracer tool. "Draw" on the fine lines of the petals, leaves and rosebuds, also using the tracer tool.

4. Patinate and polish with metal polish, and then polish with the black stove polish to enhance the blackness of the design lines.

5. Glue into position on the door.

Crafter's note

• You may find it easier to do the fine lines of the petals, leaves and rosebuds freehand, rather than working from the tracing.

Antique letter holder

This started off as an MDF laptop writing desk, which I varnished to give it a "good wood" finish. I got completely carried away designing the lid — a lovely large area with no irregularities. I sat back and admired my handiwork, only to realize I could no longer use the box as a laptop writing desk. My lid was now too bumpy for any kind of letter writing. (But hey, there are always emails.)

Anyway, I now have a beautiful "antique letter holder" or treasure box, which sits next to my very modern computer and holds all my "things" that cyberspace and hard drives cannot. This is not a technically difficult design. It will, however, take a fair amount of time. The entire design is completed in high relief.

You will need

MDF laptop writing desk
varnish (see crafter's notes)
paintbrush
sandpaper
tracing paper
soft pencil (6B)
pewter
hard board
masking tape
tracer tool or small ball tool
lubricant
3 pieces of felt
hockey-stick tool
paper pencil
beeswax and glass dropper
turpentine
cotton wool
patina
materials for polishing
glue

1. Remove the hinges, and paint the box with varnish. Allow to dry completely. Sand the entire box and lid with fine sandpaper. Apply another two coats of varnish, sanding between coats. Allow to dry.

2. Cut a piece of pewter to fit the lid of your box. Trace the design from page 143 onto the tracing paper.

3. Place the pewter, right-side up, onto the hard board. Complete the design as for high relief.

4. Fill the back with beeswax and clean off excess with turpentine. Patinate and polish.

5. Glue the pewter onto the lid of the box. Replace the hinges. Screw the hinge onto the box first; it will then be very easy to work out the position of the screw holes on the lid (see crafter's notes).

6. To balance the look of the pewter on the box, I have placed a thin strip of pewter at the top, above the pen groove. I have also placed a strip of pewter around the bottom of the box. It is more economical to cut four strips and join them at the corners. Remember to patinate and polish the strips before gluing them onto the box.

Crafter's notes

• I used an exterior varnish — the color is russet gloss.
• The decoupage MDF boxes usually have gold hinges, which do not complement pewter. Replace them with silver hinges from the hardware store; alternatively, spray-paint them black or silver.

Shoe and hearts earring box

Eat your heart out, Jimmy Choo! I found this stunning wooden box hidden in a pile on the "junk for sale" table in a watch and clock repair store. The inside is divided into small compartments, which were obviously designed to hold watch parts. It is perfect for holding earrings. The box was very grubby, so I gave it two coats of antique oak wood stain and a new pewter lid, and it is now ready for its next life. The design combines low and high relief.

You will need

a wooden box (or silver tin)

sandpaper

antique oak wood stain

paintbrush

satin-finish, water-based varnish

pewter

tracing paper

hard board

masking tape

tracer tool or small ball tool

lubricant

2 pieces of felt

hockey-stick tool

medium ball tool

paper pencil

beeswax and glass dropper

turpentine

cotton wool

materials for polishing

glue

black seed beads

set of wax sticks (see instructions on page 59)

1. Clean the box with a damp cloth to remove dust and grease. Give it a light sanding if it is a secondhand box. Paint with two coats of wood stain, allow this to dry, and then paint with two coats of varnish.

2. Cut the pewter to the size of your lid. Trace the designs from page 144 onto tracing paper. Place the pewter, right-side up, onto the hard board, and trace the design onto the pewter. (*Note: Do not trace the crisscross low-relief design on the inner shoe — it is easier to do this freehand later.*)

3. Complete the design as for high relief.

4. Fill the back with beeswax and clean off any excess wax with turpentine.

5. Place the pewter, right-side up, onto the hard board. Retrace the spiral shape on the hearts, using the tracer tool. Using the medium ball tool, indent a little hollow where the beads will be placed. (*Note: This hollow will hold the glue.*) Keeping the design on the hard board, use the tracer tool to complete the crisscross design on the inner shoe (see crafter's notes).

6. Glue the beads in place, using the wax-stick set.

7. I have glued a patinated and polished strip of pewter all around the edge of the box. You may do this as one long strip, or four separate strips that join at the corners.

Crafter's notes

• If you prefer a shiny finish on the wooden box, use a gloss varnish instead of the satin finish.

• The reason I chose to do the crisscross design on the hard board, and not on a single layer of felt as we usually do with indented low-relief, was to keep this area of the shoe very flat. If I had done this area of the design on a cloth, the shape of the shoe would have been affected. So I deeply scored the metal, rather than indenting it. The fine crisscross pattern will hold the black, and give the shoe a more three-dimensional look.

• My glue of preference for sticking the beads to pewter is clear epoxy. Mix a little at a time, because it dries very quickly.

Personalized diary

This was made as a gift for a special friend who loves gardening. The name "Colleen" has been done in raised high-relief; the tree has been done in indented low-relief. Remember, when doing wording in raised high-relief, that the words must be done in mirror image on the back of the pewter. Write the words on the tracing paper the correct way, then turn the tracing paper over to get the mirror image.

Cat trinket-tin

I cut an oval of pewter to fit the lid of an oval trinket-tin, and completed the outline of the cat (see design on page 144) in raised high-relief, the facial details in indented low-relief. Once the design had been patinated and polished, I filled the inside of the cat design with amber-colored glass paint. Run the paper pencil around the edge of the pewter design once you have glued it onto the tin, to ensure a smooth fit. These tins make delightful gifts.

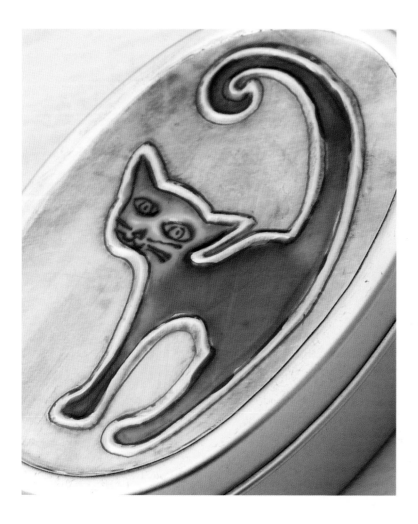

Templates

Use good-quality tracing paper to transfer your designs — the thicker, 90 gsm tracing paper is best. If you try working with thin tracing paper, the tracing tool will probably cut through it when you trace the design onto the pewter. This is very distracting, and normally results in the design being traced unevenly. When purchasing tracing paper, it is more economical to buy a larger pad of around 11" x 14" or 12" x 18" (or A3 size book) because this size will also accommodate designs for larger projects.

These designs can all be resized on a photocopier to fit the specific item you want to pewter.

In the centre of your heart is a small part & that is where your soul must go to dream.

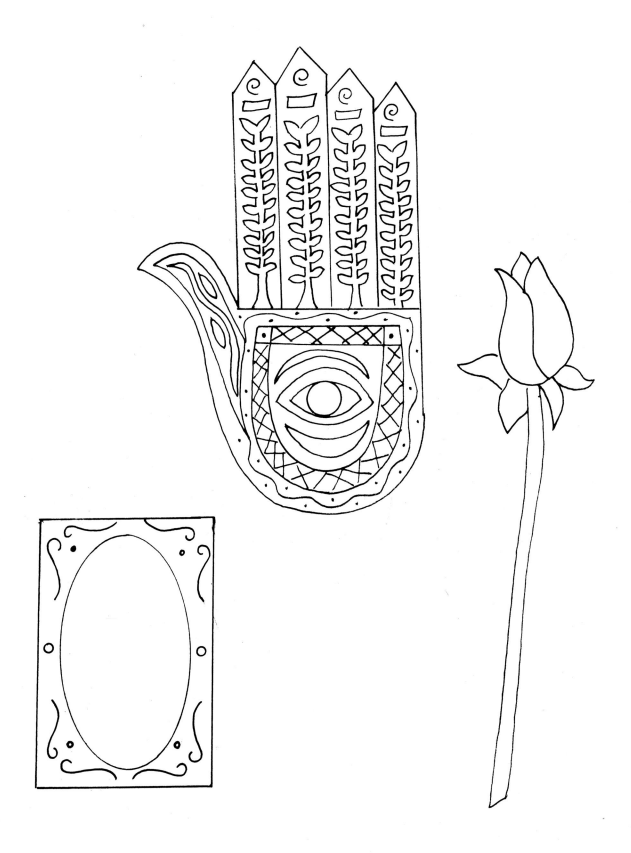

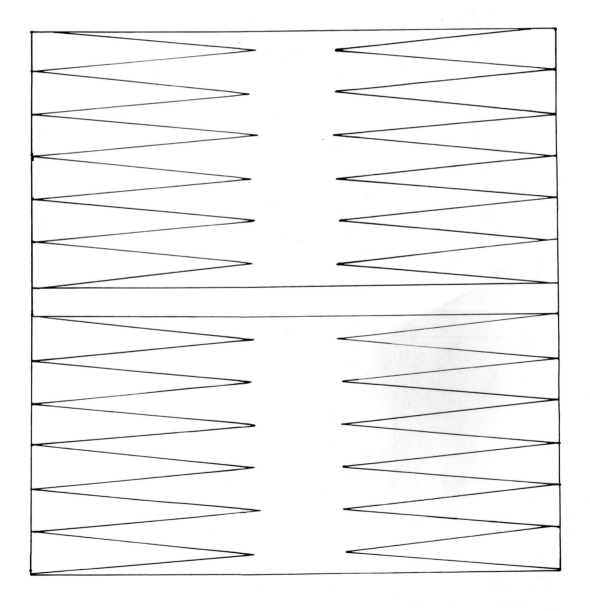

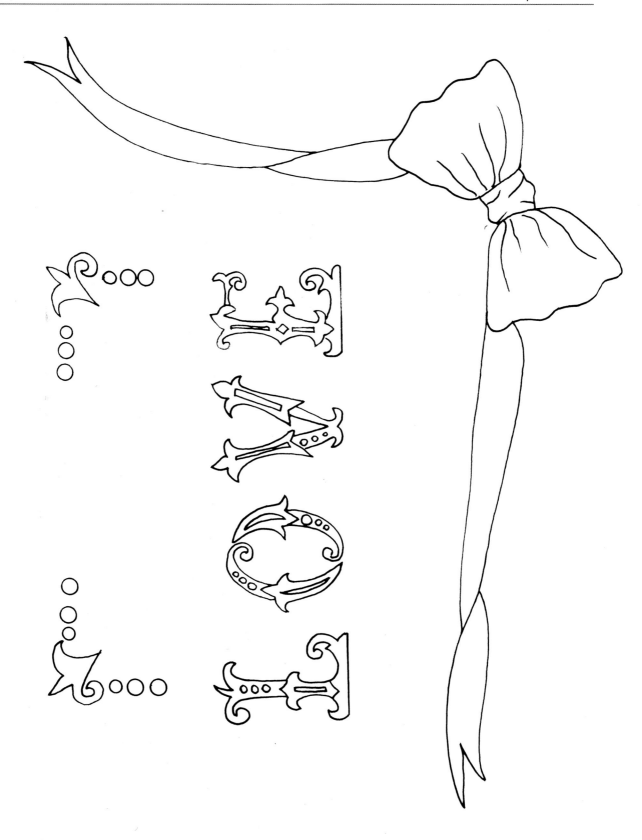

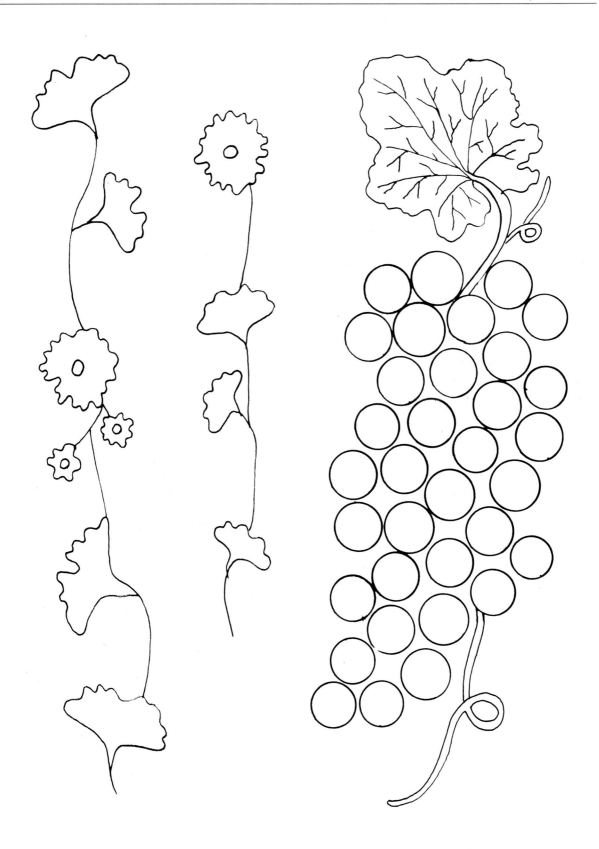

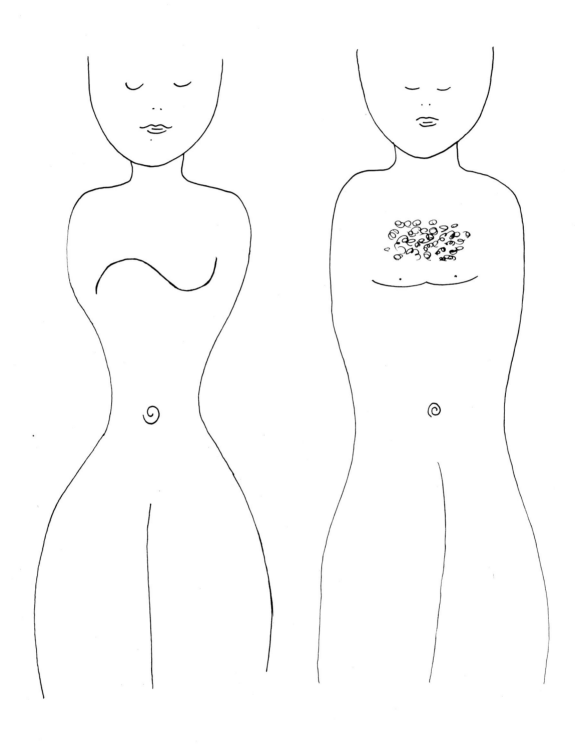